Paths Through the Year

Also by Corinne Cunningham

Farm Girl: a novel

Paths Through The Year:

A Year-long Exploration into Place, Creativity, and Self

By Corinne Cunningham

To Fynn and Paige:

may your hearts always lead you home

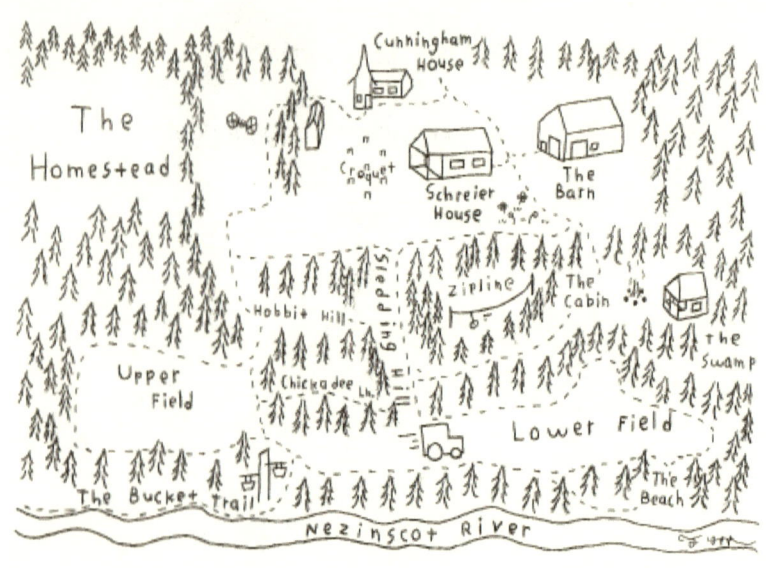

Introduction

I fell in love with lupines on a vacation to Prince Edward Island. I'd already been introduced to them by way of the children's book *Miss Rumphius* by Barbara Cooney and had seen the purple and blue cone-shaped flowers countless times over the years. But it took finding lupines everywhere I looked during a week in June on the Canadian island to fall head over heels.

A family legend from my childhood that gets told over and over is a story about a vacation to Gettysburgh in which every time we passed a cannon sitting by a wooden fence or stone wall, my mother would yell, "Stop the car!" and jump out of the passenger seat with her camera in tow before the car came to a complete stop. When we were in PEI, I was the same way, only with lupines and fences, and my kids were the ones rolling their eyes like my brother and I did all those years ago.

We were house hunting during the madness of 2021 when properties were flying off the market as soon as they became available. For years, my husband and I had wanted to move to Maine where we pictured ourselves with more space to live, breathe, and explore. Before the pandemic, we'd decided that 2021 was the year we would make the move, as we'd outgrown our tiny rental. With the flexibility of homeschooling our children combined with Lucas working remotely, it seemed like the perfect time. We started making plans and taking steps towards homeownership. Then the world shifted and changed, and everyone and their uncle were looking to move out of cities and into more rural areas.

Once we started looking at houses, I remember looking for signs, any sort of hope I could latch onto whenever we visited a property. From the outside, one of the houses we saw looked like it would be well out of our budget, but the inside - while expansive - needed a lot of work. The bedrooms were huge, there were multiple fireplaces, it had the kind of staircase and landing that you could put a reading nook into, and felt like it could be home. The backyard had a contained yet wild feeling of a secret garden, and my breath hitched at the sight of lupines hinting at blooming that dotted the backyard. Sign noted, we put in an offer that same day.

During the two days we waited to hear what happened with our offer, my father called and sprung the idea of going in on a property together, a multi-generational living situation. He knew we hadn't been able to make much traction with previous offers, and as he and my mother were looking to relocate from their home in Pennsylvania, he offered that we could join forces, knowing there would be fewer properties to look at, but hoping the demands for a multi-family property would be less than single-family homes in the current market. We said we'd have to wait and see what happened with the offer we'd just put in, but the wheels in our minds started turning. What if the offer gets accepted? What if it doesn't? What would it look like to live next door to my parents?

As you might have guessed, the offer wasn't accepted, and we said yes to the idea of multi-generational living and set out to find a very particular real estate listing. We were looking for a property with two houses, preferably detached, but we were willing to compromise. One unit for my family of four, the other for my parents. We thought a yard might be nice, but not a shared one, and it'd be great to have privacy from other neighbors. But we didn't set out to buy a big piece of land. Hay fields weren't on our bucket list. Neither was riverfront property, or woods for that matter.

Early in June we settled in for the long wait on a unicorn property, but on Father's Day weekend, we got another phone call from my dad.

3

"Did you see the listing I sent over?" he asked. I hadn't. "I think I found it," was his reply. The listing had been up for months - unheard of at that time - and there were some funky attributes, as it was listed twice with two different acreages. But what it showed got us all excited: a large amount of property, two houses, a barn, and a cabin. From the Google Maps aerial view it looked like you could see neighbors on three sides, but just barely. And beyond that? Land. Lots of land.

We contacted our real estate agent, Karen, to see if we could have a viewing set up. By midweek Lucas, myself, and our daughter were standing in the driveway of the property, being told that there were some unique things about this showing. The biggest was that the owner and his agent wanted to be present.

By this point, we'd gotten to know Karen fairly well. We'd spent a good many weekends together, traveling the back roads of Maine through snow storms, mud season, and now black flies. So when she looked at us and said "This is really unusual guys, but…" we trusted her and ran with it, and embarked on the most unusual house viewing experience we'd had to date.

We walked into the house and before we could even take in the tall ceilings, tiled floors, and the centerpiece of a stone chimney and wood stove, we met Steve, the owner, who had maps of the property laid out on the island counter top in the kitchen. As he poured over the extensive property lines laying out where the river was and how this large parcel of land had changed and morphed over time, I tried to take in the ceramic farmhouse sink and the wood beams above us. As he explained the covenants the land was included in and told us a bit about the neighbors, my eyes tried to take in every detail surrounding me: the wood beams above, the butcher block counters, the way one room flowed into another, the house seemingly endless especially compared to our current living space. Eventually, he walked us around the house, pointing out every addition and change he and his wife made during their multiple renovations. He showed us the ins and outs of the late 1800s farmhouse, then he walked us over to the little house that sat just across the way, and the barn - all the while my parents listened in via a video call on my phone.

Eventually, it was time to see the rest of the property, which included a cabin and the land. Steve offered to take our daughter around on his ATV, a four-wheeler type thing with a roll cage over top. Everyone looked at me for permission. I looked at Karen, she gave the slightest nod, and then I gave the go-ahead. Steve's realtor said he'd meet us at the cabin in his truck, where he'd then give us a ride around the fields as well, but left me and Lucas to walk for a few minutes with Karen, so we could discuss all we'd seen and our initial thoughts.

I remember Karen's excitement, she'd been with us through countless house tours that just didn't meet our needs. Prior to joining forces with my parents, most of the houses in our price range needed extensive renovations, or we'd have to give major concessions to make any of them work for us. And while the houses on this property weren't perfect - the one for my parents was much smaller than they'd wanted or imagined, and the bathroom situation in both left another toilet to be desired - the layout of the whole package was something we would never be able to find again. We walked, huddled together, talking about the strangeness of the day, and how the owner must like us if he offered to take Paige for a ride. He'd mentioned he didn't want to sell to people who didn't appreciate the property, who might split up the land. The more time we spent with him and the space, we understood.

And then we walked past a line of trees, and something in my heart shifted and would never go back. In the heat of early summer, the scent of balsam wafted across our path. It reminded me of childhood vacations up in Acadia National Park, of midnight trips to L.L.Bean, of campfires and lips sticky with marshmallows and graham crackers. It reminded me of what I wanted our lives to feel like.

And I knew.

We were home.

What came next was a whirlwind of conversations, some tears, and declining the property that I felt in my bones was home.

I remember sitting on the deck of our tiny rented home in Massachusetts, talking with my husband, listening to the constant stream of cars driving by, saying, "It's so much more than the houses. If they could just stand there and see the fields and wood, hear the river, smell those trees… they'd understand."

They, meaning my parents. Understandably, it was difficult for them to grasp the scope of the place through phone screens and hundreds of miles. But just a few days later, they came to their own knowing and decided to take a giant leap of faith with us, and make an offer that was accepted soon after.

We first visited what would become our property

in June when any signs of spring flowers had long gone. It took until the following spring for us to find out our town is covered in lupines for a few weeks of the year. They surround the welcome sign, and pop up along the side of the road like parade spectators each spring. The first plants I bought and planted around our house were, you guessed it, lupines, and they're now spread across the wildflower meadow just beyond my parent's home.

When you start looking for signs, you bring with you a view of what you think you want, and what you think you need. I'd offer that sometimes we can't see the full picture from our vantage point. Maybe there are also forces at play that we can't fathom continuously working in our favor. While there was heartbreak over the offer on the house with lupines in the backyard that didn't go through, there was also hope and excitement over what could be. Maybe those lupines in the secret garden were a sign to dream bigger, to remember the expansive feeling of being on PEI, of fields of green, and Anne of Green Gables-type daydreams and wonder. Looking back, I think it was a sign that we'd find somewhere to plant our own lupines, a sign to keep going, to keep looking, to stay the course.

Because we stayed the course, we now have a wealth of nature at our fingertips to explore. We're enveloped in the natural world and its cycles daily, and have let those ebbs and flows lead us and change our lives little by little as the months have added up to years.

What follows is the documentation of 2023, our second full year on the property we lovingly call the homestead, and an exploration of the ways in which focusing on the cycles of the seasons impacts our daily life. In particular, *Paths Through the Year* focuses on how living with and paying attention to seasonal rhythms has informed my creativity as a mother, writer, wife, daughter, and woman living in rural Maine. It is a love letter to our life and the ways we embody our days.

I make no apologies for romanticizing a quiet life, but even a chosen simple life comes with its share of joys, challenges, and sorrows. A year's worth of all three made it into this book. I hope you enjoy the unfolding of my 2023. It was a joy to document, witness, and live these twelve months, and a privilege to begin the cycle all over again as the year turns.

January

2023 starts like most recent years, my energy wanes as midnight approaches alongside my husband Lucas's while our two teenagers, sixteen-year-old Fynn and fourteen-year-old Paige, are showing no signs of fatigue. It's funny how the older we get, the more resistant we are to give up rest in the name of seeing a year turn from one bunch of numbers to the next. Maybe it's age, or maybe it's the knowledge that numbers don't hold as much value as we give them credit. Or maybe it's that this year we have house guests, and our energy has been spent visiting and entertaining. Our guests are still getting over jetlag and aren't staying up until midnight with us, so our celebrations are quiet, which doesn't help my sleepiness.

My brother and his wife are visiting from their

home in Switzerland for three weeks. They arrived at the end of December and will stay until the middle of January. It has been over four years since we've last seen Toby and Adrienne, and it's their first visit to our new home on thirty-plus acres of land we bought with our parents, who now live next door. Within that time, not only have the children grown taller, but relationships have morphed and changed, and we've all survived a pandemic.

Leading up to this visit we all felt nervous, how would it work? Three weeks is a long time, would everyone get along? We asked similar questions before our move with my parents. How would it work? We've never spent that much time with them, at least three members of my family hadn't, and the last time I had was decades earlier when the relationship dynamics between myself and my parents were drastically different.

Worry, as they say, is wasted energy, but still… there was worry. Eventually, we realized the only thing we can do is to trust and jump into living in a small town in the middle of Maine on a family compound, and to a three-week-long visit with extended family, both with our whole hearts.

When the clock turns to midnight and the calendar rolls over the moment is quiet, our guests sleeping in the makeshift bedroom in our living room, my parents next door tucked into their beds, and the four of us - myself, Lucas, and the kids - are in our sitting room watching the fireplace glow rather than a glittering ball drop on the television. We're reflecting on not only the last twelve months, but the last few years, and what's already transpired during my brother's visit.

As we sip on sparkling grape juice, my eyes dance around this room where just last week we sat around the tree on Christmas morning. That morning was full of joy and warmth. We are a family of creative people who are inspired by our surroundings. From the homemade decorations that hang on our walls made from materials found on our property, to the hand-crafted gifts that were given by all, the feeling of a connected, heartfelt, and understanding family was at our hands. We are musicians, makers, woodworkers, seamstresses, artists, bakers, knitters, crocheters, and patrons of the arts. Watching my son perform Christmas songs on his bass, I looked around at the eight of us, and my eyes glistened with tears.

And so we begin January amid nightly family dinners at our house, Mom and Dad coming over from next door, my brother and his wife entrenched in the dailiness of our lives. We spend mornings and evenings by the fire, saying little but laughing and loving and being present with our whole beings. We spend our days in a flow of togetherness, then quiet, togetherness, then apart, togetherness, and finally falling into our beds exhausted but ever so full of family and this full circle bubble we live in for three weeks.

Throughout the early part of the month it's clear that while we enjoy time spent together, all of us also need time alone. And if not alone, time together outside where the trees take up more space than we do, and the rolling hills soften any harsh edges that make their way to the surface when you put a bunch of introverts together for an extended time.

The land feels like a space that can tenderly holds us. When I walk in silence, I start writing in my head. When I grow quiet, the words bubble up and have nowhere to go but strung together, one word after the other. Sometimes I don't know where the words will end up, on a social media post, in a notebook, or here on these pages, but they always come. And they're always in my voice. Sitting at the desk in front of my computer, there are times when I write in a voice that is too thought out, too contrived, too picked apart, and layered with what I think people want to hear. It overwhelms a quieter voice, the one I know is my own.

Outside, when my body is busy trying to stay upright while navigating an uneven landscape, I'm able to hear myself think, and my words come back to me. Outside, the fresh air takes my worries and inner critic away in the breeze.

Even inside, the weather and our surroundings dictate the flow of my writing day. The cold winter days call for fires, so I bring the laptop and my notebooks to the sitting room where I can hear the fire crackle and pop and sit in the warm east-facing sunshine. On the days when the house is busier and louder, I end up under the covers and heavy blankets of my bed, computer resting on my legs or a makeshift pillow table. The wind catches on one of the window sills of the garage and it sounds like a chainsaw. The January morning light feels full and warm, and I want to soak up every last sunbeam, knowing next month it'll feel paler and thin. After the darkness of December, that's part of the hopefulness of January - the extra light to our days. It sits on the bowl of bananas on the kitchen counter and streams across the tile floors, and warms our faces when found on the trails in the woods, the trees blocking harsh winter winds.

We comment about how it feels so nice, cheeks still stinging with cold, hearts weary after the first of the year filled with resolutions and promises of change, but the days and our bodies feel the same. There's a disconnect that happens in January when our bodies want to soak in the slowness of the winter, but man-made rhythms urge you to do and move and hustle and race and achieve. That disconnect is so loud, it's almost physically painful.

Spending time in nature shows us the reality is not quite so stark. The natural world urges thoughtfulness in January, moving slower and with more intention during winter, conserving warmth and energy. For safety, you can't traipse across a partially frozen river without falling in, risking hypothermia. Resourcefulness is key, and after the extravagance of the holidays there needs to be thought about making the shed full of wood last until spring. Keeping an eye on the temperatures, the weather, and storm prep is different here than where we lived in eastern Massachusetts. Resources are acquired differently, as a trip to the nearest box store is further than a stone's throw away, and can be made challenging by weather conditions. Survival in itself is an act of creativity, and urgency is a container in which to stretch and grow, to challenge oneself.

Early in the month my husband, daughter, our Australian Shepherd Darcey, and I head out for a walk around the property. In mid December it snowed over a foot, but thanks to a few days of rain and mild temperatures most of it has melted. Some ice hangs on, mostly in the fields and through the woods that run alongside the river. With the rain and melting, riverbanks flooded into the woods and fields, leaving behind ice tables around trees. Today as we walk across frozen sections of the field we see not just the hay poking through, but a field mouse scurrying below through tunnels it has made between the layers of ice and ground below. The shadow of its body and tail fly through the tunnels with each of our footsteps. We gaze at footprints left by the wildlife - marveling over deer, some sort of feline, and turkey tracks - before heading inside to warm ourselves by the fire.

Later in the day I can't stop thinking about the mouse tunnels. If you look out at the field on any given winter day, from a vantage point of above surface level it looks like the world is asleep. Your breath carries out in front of you until it dissipates into nothing. The sound of your footsteps, breath, and maybe the wind rustling through the forest are the only sounds you'll hear.

But below the surface, there's still activity. There are still hearts beating, breaths being taken, and food stored and eaten, they just aren't as visible as the other three seasons of the year. We see animal tracks and stare in wonder, but there's a feeling of disconnect as we don't see the actual animal. Like BigFoot prints, it feels like they're part of a joke, a figment of our imagination. There can't really be large cats that roam the fields when we're safely nestled in our beds at night, can there?

Toby and Adrienne trek out to set up trail cameras one day. They come inside with tales of following tracks off the beaten path, their cheeks pink with cold. The next day they walk back out, bundled up in their woolens, only to find the temperatures dropped so much overnight that the camera battery went dead. No sightings, but we know there's life out there.

Every year there's a bit of a thaw in the first few

weeks of the year. Our photo album is full of pictures of the kids at the beach in January, pants rolled up to their knees, grins spread wide across their chubby-cheeked faces, splashing in the water. Mother nature gives New Englanders a bit of a reminder of what's to come if we can just make it through the winter. On the coast you see people flocking to the beach to feel their feet in the sand, no matter the temperature. Inland it's not so much a preview of spring beach weather, but of mud season. Boot prints overtake animal tracks on the trails, and while there are bits of ice, the majority of what you feel beneath your feet is the squish of liquid, and it takes much effort to center yourself so as to not end up covered in the stuff on the ground. Instead of sandy footprints left behind in the car from adventures to the beach, the floor mats are covered in mud. The toddlers I couldn't keep back from getting soaked in the waves now have footprints bigger than my own, and I have to coax them outdoors.

We say goodbye to Toby and Adrienne during this preview of mud season. There's a collective wish that there was more snow, comments about a mild winter, and alongside a longing to not say goodbye, a need to get back to the rhythms of our everyday life. I drive them down to the airport on a Saturday evening, and as soon as we

hit the state line that runs between New Hampshire and
Massachusetts it begins to snow. It's coming, I quietly tell
myself, fighting back tears as I drive, and there's no way to
avoid their leaving.

Halfway through the month, I find myself looking in
the full-length mirror in our bedroom, and not recognizing
the person I see looking back. It's happening more and
more. I've always loved cold-weather clothes, and I'm an
avid knitter and have a cabinet full of hand-knit sweaters
that I enjoy wearing. I love the feeling of being enveloped
by layers, it makes me feel like I'm wearing a weighted
blanket throughout the day. But as any 40+-year-old
woman will tell you, as our bodies change and shift with
age, there's a certain dysphoria that occurs, and we start to
look in the mirror less and less. How we see ourselves in
our mind does not match with what we see in the mirror.
And because I'm loathed to take on the wrinkles, my gaze
goes to what I adorn myself with, my clothes.

Before living here, it was easy to dress the way I
wanted to without considering the elements for more than
if it was warm or cold outside, and what sweater to pair

with what pants. It's the same now but with the added factor of needing to get outside regardless of the weather. Rain or snow, the dog needs to be walked. Above or below freezing, the compost needs to be taken to the pile. Walks need to happen not just for the dog, but to stave off seasonal depression, which affects more people than admit it in this part of the country. During the summer I wear tall rain boots for walks to fend off the ticks - doesn't matter what else I wear, jeans, sun dresses, shorts, the tall boots are a necessity. But in the winter it feels more complicated if I want to wear anything other than leggings. So I resort to leggings and sweaters, leggings and sweatshirts, leggings and and and… and then I can slip on a pair of snow pants for extra warmth before heading outside, or slide my feet into my boots without having to tuck my jeans in when the dog needs to go out for a quick trip around the house.

So I look the other way when I pass the mirror, afraid of what the skin-tight leggings will highlight, but feeling like there's no way around them. Part of it is not knowing how to dress at this age. And I know, trust me, I know, I should wear whatever the heck I want. But I need to also dress for the life I'm living.

The life I'm living is one of a woman who lives on a hay farm and homeschools her two teenagers; a part-time writer working from home who spends her days at home, in the fields and woods, or running kids to activities.

Leggings are perfectly appropriate for such a life.

And yet, they don't feel good.

What it comes down to, is I have transplanted my life ultimately from an oceanside city to a rural country setting, and I feel like I've lost myself in the process.

I talk to some friends about it and find that I'm not alone. It's not just the situational change, but something that has come up for many women around this age. Our bodies shift. We aren't considered young any longer, but we're also not old. And for those of us who are not constricted by a work dress code, we find ourselves floundering a bit as our style evolves and our needs are changing.

"What styles are you drawn to?" my friend Kylee asks in a text message.

I stare at the phone and think to myself, "How the hell do I know?"

Images of other women come to mind, all of whom have completely different body types than me. I'm five foot four inches with an hourglass figure that's a little less pulled in at the middle than it used to be. My legs aren't long enough to pull off high-waisted skinny jeans without pulling the eyes to places I'd rather them not. My breasts easily become the focus if I'm not careful about the shape of the sweater I throw on top of my tee shirt. I don't have the patience for shapewear, I'm trying to accept my body for what it is, and not try to wish it away or work off parts. My relationship with food has its own issues, as food allergies and intolerances have plagued me for the last two decades, and a recent diagnosis of Irritable Bowel Syndrome has me watching my stress levels as much as what I put into my mouth. All of this combines to a mess of rearranging a sense of self and reacquainting myself with who I am.

Reaching for my phone, I start to search for inspiration and end up looking at an account on Instagram that I've followed on and off for years. It's a woman who creates sewing patterns and makes most of her own garments. Her aesthetic is such that I can find an element of my own in her style here and there, but her boldness, the way she owns herself and makes clothes fit her - doesn't make herself fit the clothes - leaves me intimidated and in awe.

I send Kylee the account and say, "I love her style." My face turns red with vulnerability as I wait for her reply. It's like I'm showing a part of myself I haven't shared with anyone. I'm sharing something that I wish for myself that I don't feel is something I can pull off, not something I deserve to feel.

"I can see you in every one of those outfits," my friend replies.

And in that moment, I feel seen. At that moment, I feel understood.

"What's stopping you from picking out clothes like that?" she asks.

I don't want to answer.

In my head there's a flurry of excuses: money, practicality, appropriateness… but what it comes down to is owning myself. I keep thinking, *I'm just not ready*. But the reality is, none of us know how long we have on this earth, so why shouldn't we embrace ourselves at any and every given moment?

We end the text exchange with her holding me accountable with some next steps, ideas of where to go thrift shopping, and a promise on my end to not let myself off the hook.

Later that week I start to think about the clothes I do have and start to look more thoughtfully at my choices when I get dressed in the morning. One day, instead of throwing on a pair of leggings, I go through my pants drawer and try on every single pair - jeans, corduroy, everything. Any that feel even slightly uncomfortable, I throw in a pile. Not to get rid of, but to put away for a while, to see if I miss them. All the skinny jeans go in the pile. All the high-waisted pants are next. Moving forward, I start to take a photo of myself in the full-length mirror any time I'm wearing clothes that feel good. I label an album in my photo gallery "Feels Like Me" and within a week I start to see patterns and trends. The clothes I thought might look sloppy actually look pretty good. The clothes I love the most that I didn't wear because I feared they looked like someone else, look like me. I see a color palette unfold, a slide show of looks that I can say are my style.

There's a woman on Instagram, Stasia Savasuk, who runs Stasia's Style School. On her account and in her TEDx talk, she speaks about inside-outside congruence and dressing for the person you are on the inside. When we don't do this, we feel disconnected from ourselves, and that disconnect can lead to all sorts of feelings about the way we look, and ultimately have an impact on our self-esteem.

I've been giving myself excuses for why I can't dress the way I want. I've been saying it's impractical, the weather dictates this, the land dictates that. One of my first memories of living here is of my father teaching me how to use the zero-turn mower. The day before the lesson he said in a joking manner, "Just make sure to dress appropriately," I must have given him a funny look, so he expanded, "No dresses or anything."

I rolled my eyes and said of course not.

But really, why not?

So what if you want to wear a dress while mowing the lawn? Women have been wearing dresses while doing everything a man does for centuries, and figuring out ways to do so *safely.* Underneath the joke were valid concerns of wanting to make sure I didn't wear something that would get caught in the blades or motor, or otherwise cause me harm. But this is an example of how we have, or at least I have consistently had other people's voices in my head, jokes or otherwise, as to what's appropriate and how to dress for any occasion, what other people deem appropriate for my life, and how I blindly trust their concerns and opinions over my own.

Maybe there are ways to consider the day's work, but to still feel like yourself while making adjustments. Style isn't something that needs to be forsaken in the name of a landscape. Maybe location can enhance, inform, and inspire ou style, not take away from. I'm already starting to think about how I can adapt my choice of knitting projects through this new lens, and how I can create pieces by hand that fit this life I'm living as well as my inner self.

Personal style is one way to express our creativity, yet in my mind, it's one of the first to go in the name of a smattering of chores or errands or a rush of getting out of bed and into daily life, it's the first thing that's pushed aside in the rush to throw on layers and get outside and into the fresh air. But does it have to be that way?

In the last ten days of the month, there are three snow storms. Each one brings with it cancellations and a total of two feet of snow. After one of the storms that falls midweek, the kids and I make our way to the trail that leads from my parent's backfield down to the lower field, dubbed Sledding Hill. Paige and I drag two sleds behind us as the dog bounds ahead, trying to catch up to Fynn who is on cross-country skis. At the hill, we soon realize the snow is so heavy and deep that the sleds can't get any forward momentum, and pushing by hand makes little headway. Instead of sledding, we watch as Fynn makes some tracks, going slowly, gaining a tiny bit of momentum, and then coming to a stop not even halfway down the hill. He picks up his feet and painstakingly makes new tracks. Little by little, he makes his way down to the field.

In what seems like no time, Darcey has amassed so much snow on her undercarriage that she looks uncomfortable, even though she tries her best to play and jump and frolic, putting her muzzle in the snow and rolling around until her dark face is nearly all white. I take her home and put her straight in the bath to melt the snow balls attached to her fur.

I head back out, a pair of snowshoes attached to my feet this time, and make it to the kids just as they are getting ready to head home. So I watch them go and take my time on one of the paths on our property my father made last year. The trees hang heavy, and the path narrows with snow-laden branches. I arrive home slightly out of breath to find the kids had drug out the laundry rack and set it up by the fire, their mittens, hats, and snow pants are laid out just as I've done for them for years. They sit with cups of cocoa, the water hot for tea, and even though they're tucked into their phones they each look up and smile when I come in, their cheeks still rosy.

The last storm of the month brings with it a foot of snow topped with a deluge of rain followed by a quick drop in temperatures. A few days later Fynn and I want to head out to get some much needed vitamin D. Since the sun has been on the snow all morning, we think we might be able to get out with the cross-country skis, thinking the snow had softened enough to make some tracks. That's what happened for the first leg of our journey just past the garage, but soon the snow is ice-covered, and we head home to swap the skis for snow shoes.

Snowshoes are wonderful things, but walking in them still takes a bit of effort, especially when there's a layer of ice atop the snow. Sometimes the surface will hold your weight, and at other points, you'll crush through and end up with one foot on the surface, and the other two feet under. Fynn's snow shoes are longer than mine, so we figure that if he goes first and packs the snow a bit, his size being a factor in him not falling through quite as much as his mother, it might help me have a less jarring experience. Luckily, it works, and we walk down from the House Site to Upper Field, and then through the same trail that I walked up on my own the other day. My prints are nowhere to be found, having been filled in with heavy snow, and then covered in the seeds that fell from the trees as they were pushed down by the snowfall, and then sprung up again as it melted.

Fynn's pace is easy, his steps are thoughtful and deliberate while he takes in his surroundings. He leads the way up from the trail across the Sledding Hill and up to the cabin. He's got nearly a head on me height-wise, and I can't help but follow in wonder as I watch his lithe body flow with grace and ease as he navigates the uneven path. So much of parenting is just this, watching our children as they lead the way for us. When we push too hard, when we make them follow our paths, so much gets lost. But when we watch them, when we let them lead the way, it opens our hearts and minds to experiences and moments we would otherwise miss.

When we're out together I can't help but notice how much he notices. His pace allows for the acceptance of what is right in front of us. Sometimes when I'm out on my own, even amid the fresh air and peace of nature I get lost in my head, and my feet step faster, moving as if towards some sort of finish line. By the time I get back to the house my shirt is drenched in sweat, and my heart is beating so fast I can feel it in my head. But when I'm out with him, it's a chance to slow down and to be enveloped by the world around us. It's funny how sometimes you need someone else to show you the way to your own peace.

Near the end of the month, Lucas takes the kids out
for the afternoon. I'm left with my thoughts and Darcey,
and after a week of struggling to find a portal into my
writing, I'm looking forward to an afternoon of writing.
Snow falls gently from the sky, and when I take Darcey
for a walk I leave my phone on my desk, not thinking
we'll be gone long. I put on my favorite chunky hand-knit
hat, throw on my jacket, and don't give my flared jeans a
second thought other than that they make me feel like me.
The ends of my jeans dance out and over my winter boots
that I slide into, and off we go. We follow the snowshoe
tracks Fynn and I made the other day, and I only fall
into the snow once. It's a slow walk because I'm being
thoughtful about my steps. I don't care that the ends of my
pants are covered in snow, I know they'll dry. My breath
is even, my emotions regulated. As I write in my head I
pause to smile as Darcey runs past me and then doubles
back, jumping up on my side for approval. The lessons I've
learned in January will serve me well past winter, as long

as I can stay connected to myself, keep focus of what's in front of me, and remember to breathe in the delicious cold Maine air.

February

On the first of February, the temperature barely hits four degrees Fahrenheit. It's a midweek morning, and even though I've covered my face as much as possible, my cheeks and eyes sting as I walk out into the bright morning to take Darcey out for her morning constitutional. But the sun is bright and she is happy to nuzzle her face into the fresh powdery snow, so there isn't much to complain about. It's a new month, after what felt like a particularly long one. In saying goodbye to guests halfway through the month, it was like we lived two different lifetimes in January.

The following weekend the North East is still enveloped in sweeping cold, with record-breaking lows on Mount Washington in New Hampshire where the air temperature is recorded at -47.2 degrees Fahrenheit. In Maine, the temperatures dip dangerously low, and at the worst of it, the wind chill reaches into the negative 40s. Lucas braves the cold all weekend to take Darcey outside, who thankfully makes quick work of it even though she loves to roll around in the snow and thrives in the colder temperatures. When it's this cold she winces when she puts her paws down on the ground, gingerly lifting them almost as if on tiptoes. Lucas comes inside saying it hurts to stand outside for just a moment. Late in January, we had three heat pumps installed in the house, but even they have their limits. We stoke the fire day and night, keeping an eye on the wind, the emails from the power company, and the pipes.

The wood stove stays continually aglow for more than 48 hours, we stoke the fire before bed each night, and also utilize space heaters. When I wake up Friday morning, there are dots of frost on the wainscoting on the exterior facing wall by my bedside, where the wind blows the harshest. Next door, my parent's unheated mudroom is iced over from the inside, and the temperature hovers at zero.

Friday night they come over for our weekly family dinner, crossing the frozen tundra of our shared driveway, wisps of snow flying in dangerous swipes.

"Another win for the homestead!" is something Dad likes to say while at the same time giving two thumbs up and a grin. Whether it's a grocery run for one house when the other is quarantined, grabbing mail from the post office for one another, all hands on deck cleanup days in the yard, helping to drop a kid off at an activity when I can't be in two places at once, or borrowing a car when someone's won't start and you're in a pinch. Our Friday night dinners when we're able to walk next door to spend time with family for a night out on the town, being close enough so that even the lowest temperature doesn't put a damper on our dinner plans, garner those two thumbs up.

Tonight, my mother walks into our house and her face shines with the exhilaration of a few moments spent in the brisk weather, her cheeks and nose are rosy, reminding me of where my permanently red nose come winter time is from. Her parka is the color of cornflowers mixed with lilacs, a welcome shade of spring in the depths of winter. Such is her laughter and vibrancy, a balm for the winter blues that creep in without notice.

Days later, after the temperatures rise to a safe realm, Fynn and I strap on our snowshoes and with sights on the river we make our way out for an adventure. When we first step outside, it takes our eyes whole moments to adjust to the light of the sun reflecting off the snow. Our depth perceptions are off-kilter, and I stumbled more than once as I unintentionally dig my snowshoe into a bit of an incline. The texture of the snow across the fields is like the layers of waves that build onto one another at the edge of the ocean, where water gently laps over sand. I pause to take photos, Fynn crouches next to me to look at the waves of snow as well. Once we get to the river we see some kind of animal tracks that go from one side to the other. Neither of us is adept at identifying tracks yet, or species of any kind whether it's flora or fauna for that matter, but we think they might be feline.

As we make our way back across the open field, I catch myself laughing at the way the snowshoes clink and clank against themselves, my boots, and the snow.

"The last time I was out here on my own I kept

getting freaked out by the noise," I say to Fynn. "I kept thinking something was following me."

He laughs, a sound that forever melts my heart.

"It's interesting," he says, "when you're alone it's cause for alarm, but when you're with someone else, it's kind of amusing."

He's not wrong. How many things are like that? When we deal with them alone they're downright terrifying, but when you've got someone by your side, it's not only manageable, but you can see so many other sides of a big and scary thing.

Later that week, there's spring in the air. Our bodies don't quite know what to do with the whiplash of changes in weather, the preview of the coming months. The temps reach 50 degrees, but the kids are the only ones to enjoy the outside, as Lucas and I are struck with some illness. We were unknowingly exposed to Covid for a good length of time, but we test negative for days. Our heads are foggy, our throats scratchy.

One afternoon the kids spill inside with laughter. They walked through snow that fell in their boots, melting next to their feet. Between that and the mud and puddles of melted snow on the ground, their feet are now wrinkled like prunes. They tell us they had to stop at the cabin because their feet hurt so much, and were so cold. They are both smiling, both laughing. They're both filled with adventures and time spent bonding, whether they'd call it that or not.

Laughter is what carries us through the darker months, the swells of cold and pockets of warmth. We find tiny stashes of joy and laughter throughout the day in what feels like regular places now. Our dog's given name at the animal shelter was Bouncy. We tell that to people, and they don't understand until we ask her if she wants to go outside, and then she bounces on her hind legs at the door, yelping in excitement. At times all four of her paws are off the ground at once. We wait with the leash in hand until she calms herself down enough to sit while getting attached. These winter days she doesn't spend much time outside, but she is excited every time we ask. There are times of the day when it's routine. I can look at her and say in a certain tone, "Darcey," and then she sits and looks like a pupil ready to listen to a teacher attentively. I'll prolong the question sometimes just to see her rapt with attention. She'll tilt her head as she waits. She knows what's coming. "Do you…" I pause. She gets out of the sit position and comes over close, puts a paw on my leg, bracing herself. "Do you want to go outside?" She'll push off of my leg and into the air, yelping while keeping her gaze on me to make sure I'm getting out of my chair while she starts towards the door. At the end of a long day, it's the levity we need before climbing into bed. A reminder of some lightness. A fondness for our four-legged creature who gets extra pets on the bed while we drift off to sleep.

On Valentine's Day, I wake up before dawn. The sky grows lighter, and pale pinks and yellows fill the windows. There was a dusting of snow overnight, and after a few days of mild, nearly spring-like weather, we're reminded that we're still in the grips of winter. The trees look sugar-coated, and with no wind, the snow has stayed put, creating picture postcards from Maine right on our doorstep.

There's a process to caring for knitwear, and it starts as soon as you bind off the last stitch. Your newly knit garment needs protecting from the world, or just moths. But first, there's the job of soaking. I fill a sink or the bathtub - depending on how large the project is - with water and a drop of gentle wool wash. Then I press the garment into the sudsy water and watch the hues of dye grow darker. This process is magic - so long as you don't agitate your project too much in the water.

After, you gently take your work out of the water, squeezing as much water as you can out of the sodden fiber. Next, you spread the garment carefully on a laid-out towel, roll it all up, and walk, jump, or hop over it. For a sweater, I repeat the towel process with a second towel, for socks just once will do. What you want to accomplish is taking as much water out as you can, so as you lay it out to dry the sweater dries faster and doesn't sit in a puddle of water for too long.

The last step is to lay out the sweater on blocking mats - foam puzzle piece type blocks, the ones used to line play areas for children work just fine, as does a trash bag, but never a towel. Towels will absorb the water but have a difficult time drying with the sweater on top, making for musty-smelling wool. Depending on the piece, whether lacework or if the garment needs to be adjusted size-wise a bit, you can either lay it out flat and walk away, or pin it into place so it will take on a specific shape when it dries.

This process, called blocking, smooths out wonky stitches, allows for the yarn to bloom and soften, opens up lace patterns, illuminates cables, and transforms the garment from a bunch of stitches to a finished hand-knit piece of wearable art.

Kind of like writing, once the first iteration of the product is done, it needs time to rest, to stretch. You need time to breathe more life into it, and distance to let it become what it's meant to become.

The process takes longer in winter. Even when the air is dry, the inevitable cold prolongs the drying period, a winter weight sweater may take three days to fully dry rather than one unless it sits dangerously close to the fire.

Currently there's a sweater blocking. It was cast on January 31st, and completed while watching the Super Bowl. It's a sweater made entirely of Maine wool. The yolk has a design that makes me think of Nordic ski wear, and thick sweaters that don't need a jacket over them even in the depths of winter. It's one that while I was knitting, I knew would feel good to wear, and looking at it on the blocking mats, I know it's a piece that was chosen intentionally, and that will fit my body and style, as well as checking all the boxes that come with living here.

I would like to tell you that I don't normally pump out sweaters every two weeks, but looking back on my knitting history, I do in mid to late winter. There's an urgency when I cast on and off the last of the winter projects. Like the weather is reminding me that my days of wearing the thick, weighted blanket-feeling type sweaters are numbered. Winter feels like a time of being held, to me. We create our days around the weather, the snow can inhibit plans, and yet the only limiting factor of our creativity, our daily lives, is ourselves. Our mental capacity for so much changes with the lack of sunlight, the change in Vitamin D levels. Our stores of energy, of creativity, are affected by the fatigue and downright slowness of February.

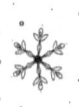

The sunrises this time of year take on a new level of beauty. I rise early and write with a community of writers online. Looking up from my work for a moment I see my face on the screen, my little box shows the hints of a sunrise. Mirrored back at me, it takes my breath away. I turn to look out the window, and it's even more gorgeous in person. There are oranges and greens, and deep blues that fade to black. It takes seeing my view through a different perspective, a different lens, to give it credit and appreciation.

And yet, it's not all snowshoeing unicorns and glittering frosty magic. The treads on my boots have worn thin over the years and on a mid-day walk around the property I slip and fall on snow-covered ice. I land ungracefully on my elbow and left hip, sending reverberations through the entirety of my back for a few days. Icy hot lotion becomes my frenemy, it tingles and cools and burns, and the scent of wintergreen lingers on our bedsheets. We're in the midst of a cost of living crisis worldwide, and our electric bill for the new heat pumps takes my breath away as much as the winter sunrise, but it leaves a much different feeling in my chest. The cost of groceries has risen across the globe, but they seem particularly high here in central Maine.

Fynn and I make a trip down to where we used to live on the northern coast of Massachusetts for an orthodontist appointment, and when we drive past our old road, our old landlord's house, and visit our old grocery store, pangs of homesickness crash over like a tidal wave. It's in the familiarity, the longing for something known. We've lived a year and a half in our small rural town, and while I can get to the places we visit regularly, I still need to check the GPS for anywhere outside of the norm. Transitions take time.

At Market Basket where prices are always lower than other stores, the price differences from home are remarkable. While living in Massachusetts we thought our cost of living was stupendous. For housing maybe, but groceries? Maine has them beat. It's a combination of transportation costs, lower population density, and access.

While driving home the further we get from the high population and congestion, the easier I start to breathe. The cost is worth it, tenfold. It's worth it for the way the light shines over the coffee table each morning and the peace that comes with looking out back and seeing only my parents. The sky feels vast and open, and while at first that somehow felt claustrophobic compared to standing on the shores of the ocean, it now feels like something I couldn't live without. The thick tree lines, the ice that looks like mosaics on the river edge, the waves of snow across the field, they all inspire as much awe and as many streams of words that beg to be written as the ocean ever did.

By mid-month the conversations during Friday night dinners turn to the fields. Dad asks if we've been down to the river, and the kids tell their grandparents about their trek earlier in the month. They talk about the height of the river, and the depths of the snow.

Dad shakes his head, crosses his arms over his chest, and says "It's going to be a while." He's putzed as much as he can putz in the barn. There's new equipment that he's itching to try out. When Toby and Adrienne were here, Adrienne - who works in forest conservation in Switzerland - helped us tag some trees and shed some light on how we can work with the forest to promote growth and health in the ecosystem. It will be a lifelong project, and my father can't wait to get started. But there's also the weekly maintenance of the property, the mowing and weed whacking, the garden projects he and Mom are eager to begin and continue, the mowing along the edges of the fields, and of course, seasonal and storm clean-ups. There are never-ending lists, and in the depths of February they're the stuff of daydreams and heart songs.

Late in the day on the 18th, we take Darcey out for a walk. Chickadees follow us with their songs as they dip in and around the trees. Turkey prints dance on top of dwindling snow. The week has been mild, and so there are expanding areas of pine needle-covered dirt. A false spring lured us into some kind of comfort just days ago, but the temperature dipped again and we've felt the chill deeper in our bones and stayed close to the roaring fire well into the evening even as the golden light kisses the tips of the trees, promising more to come in the coming days and months. For the first time this year we notice the golden hour light is later than it has been and when we arrive home at just before five, the darkness is nowhere in sight, the need for the fire is a memory quickly forgotten in the name of hope.

Since the new year, I've found my reading slowing. With the turn of the year came loads of nonfiction titles that I wanted to go through, and I read them morning and evening. Usually, I stick to fiction in the evening, but nothing has piqued my interest. This led to reading about topics like self-compassion right before bed. Not a bad thing, but it sets my mind to working overtime, thinking about how I could use the information, and letting it process. The ways of winter catch up with me, and I start falling into bed earlier and earlier, so tired I can't even pick up a book. Eventually, I start craving stories again and pick up a handful of novels without too much thought at the library. The more colorful the cover, the better. The simpler the plot, the more I'm drawn to it. Happily ever is the way stories make their way back to my heart.

And at the same time, after several months of having stepped away from my fiction writing, I start to feel the characters and stories bubble up. They whisper to me when I'm on a roll with the writing of this book, when I read novels, and they are starting to show up as I write in my mind on daily walks and long car rides. It makes me think there's something to giving space for what's calling, and letting what needs to fade into the background grow fuzzy.

There's another few days of fake spring. Mud takes over the paths, and everywhere we drive we see piles of dirt and sand-covered snow. There's another 5-8 inches in the forecast for the end of the week, and while I hear some grumbles over it, my heart quickens at the thought of fresh snow. This time of year while I appreciate the warming temperatures, I am even more thankful for the dip back into winter. Winter feels like a season of cocooning. In a way, the elements drive us inward and feel like a security blanket, a reason to stay inside, a force for togetherness with the family.

And yet, the wide swings of temperatures - even the scents of spring in the air - are starting to wear on me. The back and forth, the never knowing how many layers to wear, adds to the frustration over clothing I felt last month. I want to see myself, and it's hard to find myself under layers.

The day before the snow comes I swing by my parent's house. The conversation about the storm feels more subdued than others this winter, more utilitarian, and it has more of a get-the-job-done mentality. Dad's tractor is kitted out with a snowblower attachment on the front and a blade on the back, and it's had an oil change and all its fluids checked. It's rote now, the conversation and the maintenance. On our daily walks, we slip and slide more than walk, the snow has melted into ice that's slick any which way you go at it: digging your heel in first, with metal grips attached to the bottom of your boots, stamping down hard with every step. I search out uncovered ground, as does Darcey. Her paws and my boots get muddied, but at least we're on steady ground. If winter is truly not letting up, we need a fresh batch of snow to not only ease the eyesore that is dirt-covered snow but also for our boots to grip. Even if we know there are still layers of ice below.

The day of the storm I'm out with the dog first thing in the morning. It's that time before the sun even hints at being up and the world looks blue. Snow falls gently, the wind is stirring. There's a good three inches on the ground, and Darcey wants to play. She sniffs and snuffles in the snow, then lays down and looks at me expectantly. No, I tell her, I won't lay down. Sometimes I do, and then she comes over and sits in my lap while looking at the world around us. Because of those rare occasions, she gets her hopes up every time. I wonder why I don't, and then I remember: inside, the kettle's on, and I'm wearing pajama

pants and Lucas's shoes that slide on - they're oversized
on me and snow has already made its way around my heels.
Reluctantly, Darcey follows as I walk towards the door,
and I whisper promises of play that get lost in the wind as it
whips around the corner of the garage.

We don't make it outside until late afternoon. After
being somewhat unwell again, a wave of fatigue has hit.
My hip and lower back are still reminding me of the fall
on the ice earlier in the month. I feel February, the very
essence of it, in my bones. While January and February are
both seated in the heart of winter, February feels the most
like the depths of winter. This year it's especially true with
the nosedive in temperatures, howling winds, and teases
of spring only to be reminded that no, you've still got
quite a bit of the season left. Even for someone like myself
who enjoys reasons to stay home and be cozy, by the end
of February, my heart aches for warmth, for crocuses, for
fewer layers. It clings to the hope that flies on chickadee
songs and lingering daylight.

It's mid-afternoon, and Paige and I are both sitting
by the fire. The dog stirs from her corner of the couch, and
I ask Paige - rather half-heartedly - if she wants to go for a
walk.

"Sure," she says, "let me get ready."

I can't even muster a smile, and rousing myself from my well-worn seat on the couch where I've spent most of the day feels like moving through quicksand, but Darcey heard the "w" word, and is already shaking off her nap and moving towards the door. I feel like I need to shake a bit off, myself. Earlier in the day a friend told me it sounded like I had a shift to make, she wasn't wrong, but every inch of my body and mind resists.

Such is February, the month that could be labeled resistance.

On come the layers: snow pants, extra socks, boots, the metal grippy things you put on your boots, thermal shirt, sweater, winter coat, hat, and gloves. I'm already tired, and I've only gotten dressed. The couch looks so inviting, the fire is so warm. What are we thinking, going outdoors?

Darcey bounces and bounces, and out we go. The storm lingers, and so the sky is not the brilliant blue that can trick us into believing it holds warmth. No, it's overcast, and snowflakes fly around us. But the air is fresh and a few steps in, the work of walking with layers and layers on gets the heart pumping and soon I forget it's not even 20 degrees Fahrenheit.

I look over at Paige who decided not to wear snow

pants. She doesn't even have mittens on, instead, her hands are shoved into her pockets. The only time I see even a hint of regret about that decision is when she tries to climb a tree, and the limbs are covered in snow. She shakes her hands to rid them of cold clumps, but then says something about the sap that's lingered on her hands - something about it being easier to wash off of hands than mittens. I pick my battles. I knew we wouldn't be out for very long, though to be honest she made it out of the house gloveless without my knowledge. I feel a brief sting of guilt but then my thoughts trail off into the wind that's now stirred up around us.

Darcey tries to tunnel in the snow, she rolls around in it and waits patiently while we navigate icy patches. Sledding Hill looms up ahead, and most days I can feel how the practice of going uphill at least once daily has strengthened my legs, my muscles, and even my heart. But today, it feels like a slog. The dog bounds up, barely slowed by the six inches of powder she pushes through, Paige close at her heels. I trail behind. I'm holding the long lead Darcey's attached to, and so I'm no more than 30 feet away from the pair of them, their pace has slowed and I can feel impatience build. Finding my footing on snow and mud-covered ice, and then another layer of snow has me walking with caution to an extreme. The weight of the day, the month, the layers and layers, I feel it all as I climb this hill, one foot halfway in front of the other - not even a full step. More like a shuffle. I huff and I puff, and we take a break at the top.

"You're not even winded? Just a bit?" I ask Paige. She shakes her head with a slight smile, "Not really." She follows up with a shrug, the kind I remember giving when I was fourteen. "It's no big deal" is what the shrug suggests, "sorry it is for you," is what it means. There's empathy in her eyes, and it tugs at a soft spot in my gut, but I push the feeling away and all I can see is her barely zipped coat, her rosy cheeks, the smile that still catches me off guard since she got her braces off a few months ago. This young woman, so full of life and zest, it's been a heavy month for her, too, and yet here we are, outside. Together.

Darcey pulls at the lead, telling us she's ready to go home. The last bit of the walk is the most unprotected from the wind, and we all walk slowly as the wind pushes and pulls us in all directions. By the time we make it to the house, we're breathless, even Paige, and tumble inside, kicking snow from every inch of our boots, the dog licking the clumps that have accumulated between her toe beans and paw fur. Our cheeks are windburned, and my nose drips as it defrosts thanks to the roaring fire while I'm taking off layer after layer.

There's never been a walk I've come inside from and said, "I shouldn't have gone," and similarly, there's never been a writing session where I've ended and thought, "I shouldn't have sat down to write" But the energy it takes for both actions - walking and writing - are at points hard to muster. Especially in February. The inertia for almost all things has slowed. It takes longer to get places, it takes more effort to move, it takes more thought to do just about anything. Movement and writing are inextricably linked for me. When I'm outside and start moving the loud voices within are busy keeping my body safe in the outdoors. Once I get started, momentum builds, and it's like I'm filled with a lightness, even a sense of joy, that comes with the work of finding words to express myself, to express what I see around me, and yes - to make sense of it all.

A feeling of wanting to sleep until spring blankets our household on the last day of the month when we're gifted with another few inches of snow. Instead of giving into it completely, I make a cozy nest of blankets and shawls in my writing chair. From my writing desk, I can see what looks like gently falling confectioners sugar, and what it means for me is more time here, less time rushing to errands and trekking to and fro for the kid's activities. I want more of these magical snow-filled mornings where I can curl up with my words and imagination, and not feel the tug of the outside world. That's the joy of winter for me.

How many of us wish that we could close our eyes, and magically wake up past mud season and into flower-studded walkways and meadows filled with bees and butterflies? It's not that we're fighting against our nature, humans weren't hibernators to begin with. We survived winter with fire, shelter, and clothing. And while we didn't sleep through winter, we did slow down. We did prepare. And if our reserves weren't filled, well, no one would want it to come to that. But there are times when we have to dig deeper and find the extra canned goods that are hiding behind the empty jars that sit in wait for sun-kissed preserves.

What February reminds us, especially one with temperatures all over the map, is the push and pull of living seasonally as humans. The push of our drive of production, and the pull of nature's rhythms. We are called to coexist, lean into flexibility, to bring our sensibilities and survival instincts to our days while incorporating the wonder of the wild world around us.

March

March comes in like a lion with a weather pattern of a storm descending on us every other day. On our daily walks we find places where the snow comes up past our knees. It feels like a never ending pattern of snow storm, blue sky day, snowstorm, blue sky day, repeat… and the worries we had about a light snow winter earlier in the season, and last month's hopes for an early spring, have both disappeared under the multiple feet of snow we've received.

For the first two months of the year, I focused my writing time purely on the seasons, cycles, and our daily life. I put aside work on my novel in progress back in October, having gotten myself into a confused and slightly burned out state of being with my fictional worlds. Recently, a group of friends and I have started working through Julia Cameron's *The Artist's Way,* and while I thought I was already doing "morning pages," after reading about her process, I realize I've forgotten one key point: to keep the pen moving. In another turn of phrase it's called free writing, a practice I learned in a creative writing class in high school, and something I spent time teaching in writing classes for adults as well as in the courses I facilitated within homeschool co-ops for all ages of children. But over the last few years, I stopped calling it free writing, and started focusing on journaling. Journaling, to me, felt like a more thoughtful process, more meandering than the slap dash hurry of free writing. Free writing, at its very core, is keeping your pen moving across the page at all costs. If you don't know what to write about, you literally write "I don't know what to write." It's a way of turning off our sensors, a way of getting past what you think you should write, to simply write.

The first weekend of the month brings more intense

weather, this time in the form of 17 inches of fresh snow. The storm starts in the wee hours of Saturday morning, and by lunchtime a foot has accumulated. It falls in hefty chunks of snowflakes stuck together, but when we step outside it feels like walking through powder, though even a foot of powdery snow can feel heavy. We take Darcey outside multiple times. There's hardly any wind, and the temperatures stay mild. She tunnels and burrows in the snow. She's an anxious dog, and by this point of winter, we have to watch our patience levels. The sound of snow settling on and then falling off of our metal roof sets her on edge, and after a week of storms we're all tired and weary of her trembling body. But walks help. Being outside helps. As she bounds through the snow she leaves bits of her worry behind, making a nap possible which in turn often wipes the worry plate clean.

Because of the depths of the snow, anyone walking any distance not on a plowed path needs to wear snowshoes. Even in snowshoes, we sink to our knees, and the first pass through the unmarked snow brings aching hips from lifting our knees and feet up past our waist in order to inch forward. After that first go, we stick to our made-by-foot path, and the going is much easier. Darcey stays mostly by our side, the landscape is well known but looks so different. From our packed down path the snow on either side is well past her shoulders, a daunting feat even for our girl who likes to blaze trails and lead us instead of us leading her.

On one of our walks, we run into my father. He's been in his element, clearing snow with the tractor, but his sights are firmly set on spring.

"This should be it," he says.

I put my finger up to my lip. "You know there's been snow in April," I tell him.

We banter back and forth, and I relent, agreeing that hopefully this should be the last big storm. All we can do is wait and see. While we had snow last year, it wasn't anything like we've had these last few weeks. Last year whenever the weather reports indicated several inches we'd be lucky to get two inches. And so I've long given up on assuming the weather reports are anything but suggested outcomes, and try to take each day's forecast as it comes.

By the time I realize I've been writing morning pages every day for over two weeks, I'm starting to see how they work. While at first I feel like I'm dumping all the crud in my brain onto the page in incoherent streams of thought, as the days go on I'm accessing what's behind the filters and sensors easier. I'm finding enjoyment not only in the way ink from my fountain pen glides across the paper, going from shiny to dry within seconds, but I'm also enjoying the benefits of seeing what I actually think about things. It's as if the layers are shedding. Of myself or of winter, it's hard to say.

The sweater that was on the blocking mats last month has now been worn a handful of times, and after the latest storm it's finally in its intended element. I wear snow pants and gloves, a hat and cowl, but nothing over my sweater. There's a gentle wind, but at points it dies down and the sun warms me to the point where the sweater is almost too warm, the jacket I left at home would have made it sweltering. It's a Sunday and Lucas joins me and Darcey out on the trails, she goes from one of us to another, we stop countless times to play with her, watching her bury herself in the snow. Lucas throws snowballs up in the air and after a winter of such play Darcey still doesn't know what to do with them. We laugh, listening to the wind whistle between tree limbs. In the wooded areas it looks like there's another snowfall, the snow that caked the evergreens falls through needles that act like a sieve, fine powder falling in bunches and drifts.

"Absolute bliss," I tell myself as we walk through an opening into the sunshine. My furry friend at my side, husband behind me, sunshine on my face, the perfect choice of a handknit sweater for warmth without the swishing sound of my winter coat, this is bliss. This is joy. And in this moment I choose to embrace it, to let it wash over me, to feel it in every fiber of my being.

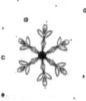

On another sunny day, I take the long way home from a walk and swing by the cabin. It's a one room off-grid building that sits on a hill overlooking Lower Field. The outside is sided with camouflage siding, but inside it radiates warmth from the honey colored logs that frame the walls and the beams above. One side of the cabin consists of a giant window that looks out over the field, to watch as the deer graze or notice the birds in the trees just outside. I've spent many a moment watching a red-bellied woodpecker from a rocking chair while sitting by the propane stove that sits in one corner. It's a shared space, and we've all taken turns escaping to the cabin. Fynn takes his bass, Paige will lug either her guitar or a set of watercolors, and Mom and I have taken our knitting and talked for hours. The cabin has seen outlining a novel, podcast recording, hand quilting, a New Year's Day game marathon fueled by leftover Christmas cookies, a 13th birthday slumber party, and countless peaceful moments with someone needing a respite from the rest of the world.

There's a porch where you can see the expanse of the area, and in the winter you can just about see through the tree line down below where the river sits on the other side. Last fall, Dad and Lucas built a fire pit for us all to enjoy. Dad brought his tractor out and dug a hole where they layered concrete cinder blocks to form a base and surrounded it with boulders and rocks found around the cabin. The previous owner left plastic fixings for three benches that could be turned into half of a picnic table each - put two together to form a whole - and Dad and I fixed slabs of wood to the plastic, and now there's three benches that sit around the fireplace. They're currently under a few feet of snow, but come spring time we'll make use of them once again.

As I walk around the cabin I remember we only

used it a handful of times this last season. I wonder why I haven't made more use of it. Not just in the depths of winter, but in any season. When people ask if the cabin serves as a writing space, I say no and fall back on the excuse of it being a shared space. I don't want to take up too much of it, time or space wise. It's someplace that is used by all - though seldom.

When I'm sitting at home and think of the cabin, there's this funny feeling of it being so far away when it's actually so close, like the feeling when a story is just out of reach, the ability to write it or piece it together feels unattainable.

But the truth of the matter is, I don't need all that much stuff to write. Given the wonders of technology and battery powered laptops, I don't even need electricity. The bathroom, sure, that's a reason, but the house is a five minute walk away and it wouldn't be the worst thing to stretch my legs now and then.

In this season, I'm overwhelmed by the ways I am my only obstacle. When it comes down to it, I am the only one blocking my own way. In writing and other areas.

The sun grows warmer each day, and while there's still snow on the ground the daily melt increases. There's another snow storm predicted, but there's something about the end of season snows, we bounce back from them quicker. While the dreariness from a mid winter storm can last days, a nearly spring storm is simply a blip on the radar.

Winter has felt like a safe season, a confined season where the world stays at bay because of cold and snow and ice. While it's a time for ideas to hibernate, percolate, this year in particular it was a season of reestablishing routines and rhythms. The upcoming season feels like an opportunity to see how they stand up, see how they really work alongside the opening up of our world, if they'll expand to the rhythms that include other people and plans on the homestead.

The predicted nor'easter hits much of New England, but somehow we're spared the worst of it. While parts of New Hampshire are walloped with over two feet of snow, we make out well with six or seven inches. It's the wet and sticky kind of snow, and the day after the storm I look out of our office window and notice that it appears like there's skeletons of the trees on the bark. There's lines of snow that have stuck to the tree trunks, from the ground level up at least two stories high.

At the midpoint of the month I wake up on the wrong side of the bed. Everything feels horrible. The dog is upset by the snow coming off the roof and tries to climb into a kitchen cabinet, pushing a glass mixing bowl off the shelf. It shatters across the floor. I yell and the dog cowers and then she climbs up into my arms as I try to keep her away from the shards of glass while Lucas grabs the vacuum. Later on when I take her for a walk through the new fallen snow, a strap on my snowshoe falters and I trip over myself and land in the snow. The day goes on, one of the kids proclaims something about the way we live our lives, and it hits me so wrong I feel my defenses pull up. I look out the windows and can't see the beauty that's right in front of me. I feel like a spoiled brat who doesn't appreciate what she has, but can't talk myself out of wishing I was anywhere else but here.

By the end of the day I'm still harboring resentment over my teenager, but right before my head hits the pillow I realize I haven't hugged them goodnight, and so I go up to their room and bury my face in their hair while giving a hug, smelling the scents of shampoo and deodorant, hay from the rabbits who live upstairs with the kids and hints of tortilla chips that have gone stale in an open bag.

"You picked a hell of a day to push my buttons," I say, and we both fall into laughter. It's not the first time, and won't be the last.

That day coincides with a downward spiral in my attitude about my creative life. It shows up in subtle ways: a lessening desire to sit down at the desk, feeling distracted and like a butterfly flitting from flower to flower, finding ways to procrastinate - especially ones that sound productive.

It's like not giving myself time out at the cabin. There's something about being my own worst enemy, my own worst block. Three months into this year-long writing project, and multiple years into fiction writing, I'm still looking for an escape. But an escape from what, exactly? And an escape to what, exactly?

Mom and I escape down to the coast where my in-laws have a condo that they use during the summer months, but as it sits mostly empty for the rest of the year, we're able to take advantage of it for quick getaways. We don't plan to stay long, just two overnights, but it's just enough. Sometimes, even when you love where you live, it's important to get away. For perspective, for inspiration, for a breather. We spend our time knitting and quilting, grabbing a bite to eat at a favorite restaurant in Kennebunkport. The sun is shining throughout our stay, and we walk the loop out to the marsh and back at the Rachel Carson Center. We stop and take selfies, our noses and cheeks are rosy, our smiles are wide and our eyes crinkle at the same places. The path is snowy and we're cautious on patches of ice, but the trail is worth the time as our lungs fill with sea air and the views of the icy marsh are so full of depth, it moves us to silence.

We also stop at a local yarn store, where we spend more time telling stories than looking at the yarn. The store keeper stops by a few times, and finally we tell her that we're busy telling family secrets, but we'll get to the yarn eventually. "Enough said," she says with a smile, and lets us get back to our stories.

Even though we live next door to each other, these

visits are never boring, and we never run out of things to talk about. And if we did? The yarn would fill in the blanks.

The last full weekend of winter, the season gives us days with endless sunshine and favorable temperatures. Fynn and I take our snowshoes out for a trek through the woods and find that in some areas the snow is packed and dense, in others there's two feet of slush and our snowshoes cut through quickly, landing us on our knees in the depths. We go slowly, as there is no other way through the slush, and come up to the cabin. When the path becomes muddy and the ground cover turns to clumpy grass mixed with mud we take the snowshoes off, and hear the sodden ground squish beneath our boots.

At the cabin we sit in the green wooden rocking chairs that witnessed the season in its entirety. They overlook Lower Field and the breadth of land the cabin sits upon. Once we're seated, neither of us say a word. The birds sing a song of the coming spring. There's a faint hum of snowmobiles in the distance. Wind seems to swish the wispy clouds away to give the blue sky full stage. And the trees, the trees are what catch my eye.

Even a week ago it felt as though we were still firmly in stick season - the trees and their branches forming straight lines out from itself and one another. But now there's more substance to the branches, my eye stutters over the fullness. There are buds forming on the tips and edges, filling limbs with potential. At first I think it's just one tree, or the ones that are firmly in the sunshine, but when my gaze scans the tree line every one of the trees is pregnant with tiny signs of spring.

We're lost to our daydreams when Lucas and Darcey come upon us at the cabin, Darcey leaps up onto the porch and greets us with her muddy paw prints landing on our pant legs. We sit for a spell as she explores, and then Fynn heads home, but Lucas and I continue on a walk. We head down the Sledding Hill and across Lower Field, trying to flow with the way our snowshoes sit atop the snow and then suddenly plunge. It's jarring, but after a few months of such walks it feels like a well orchestrated Vinyasa Flow you'd find in a yoga class.

Just as we all need a break, we come across a downed tree limb. It looks as though it's been down since at least the last storm, as it's immovable and covered in snow. The branches reach up as high as my shoulders, and upon closer inspection, it's covered with buds just like the upright trees that surround us.

Some of the buds have gone so far as to become furry, the next stage in their process. They're unfurling step by step, reaching towards the sunshine, yet untethered from the source.

We stop, and I linger over the furry buds. When I get home I try to identify the tree, I find it's a poplar. Once again, my identification skills are lacking, and my confidence has no weight. But in the middle of the field, the name of the tree didn't matter. The identification of it wasn't worth anything to me. What mattered was that it was there, and we witnessed its beauty before it's swept up into the life cycle of a downed tree limb, before it gets tossed back into the woods or into the wood chipper to become mulch for the gardens around the house. It did not matter what someone has named it, or what it will become. In that moment, it mattered simply that it existed.

On the Spring Equinox it's seventeen degrees Fahrenheit when I wake up. The sun is shining, but there's frost covering the car windshield, and the heat pumps work relentlessly through the morning.

Back in 2021, shortly after moving here, we started a pool to see who could guess when we'd get our first six inches of snow. The winner got to use a mug we had custom made which wields the title Liquid Crystalline Prognosticator Extraordinaire, from the date of the first six inches of snow until the first day of spring. That first year it took until February to crown a winner. Each of our initial dates passed by, and we had to put in another round of guesses. We got snow, but none of it came to a total of six inches in one storm until that fateful day when Lucas won the title and the mug for a few weeks before the turn of seasons.

This winter I won the mug with a date falling before Christmas. The storm was swift and the snow fell deep, and yet was gone quickly, as happens with early December snow.

Now, on this first day of spring, I prepare to give up the mug until the next winner is crowned. Holding it, I find myself lost in memories from when Toby and Andrienne were visiting. They hadn't even gotten over their jet lag before I made it known that they could not in any circumstances use this one mug, how it was extra special and I'd won it with my cunning weather knowledge and expertise, my voice dripping with false sincerity.

I scrub and scour it to remove the tea stains that have amassed from three months of use. If you didn't know any better you'd think it might be merchandise from the movie Frozen, there's snowflakes and faint blue stars around the mug, and a gigantic snowflake on one side that says "Est. 2021", Liquid Crystalline Prognosticator Extraordinaire spelled out on the other. It feels like a mug you'd find at a diner, the chunky ceramic kind that can take a beating and hold enough caffeine to get the day started on the right foot.

We try to make the hand-off a big deal, a practice in ceremony. But today, the urge to clear all the clutter and start anew with the fresh season takes over, and I walk over to my parents, swinging the mug dangerously by the handle. The box it lives in for three seasons of the year is somewhere in the depths of my mother's stashes and stores of holiday goods, seasonal decorations, and general magic making tools.

I knock on the door and let myself in, as I've been instructed to do since the day we moved in next door to one another. It was one of those things that I had to be told a few times before it sunk in. Yes, it's my parents house, but it's not the house I grew up in, and when they first moved in it didn't smell like them. It didn't smell like their home.

It wasn't familiar the way every one of their other houses had become over the years. One marker of my childhood was moving every few years, others are the scent of moving boxes, the muscle memory that kicks in when packing up books and treasures, and the way an empty house feels before you make it your own. When the turn of seasons hits, and the urge to clear and declutter arises, sometimes I have to sit and decipher between the desire to have a clean space, and the desire to move house completely.

Inside my parents house I shout out to see if anyone's home. The lights are on, and the beds are stripped, the washing machine is going. I leave the mug unceremoniously on their kitchen counter and then I head outside to investigate. I don't want to linger, while I've been told I can use their house if ever I want to get away from mine, I still feel funny about being there without them, even though it now smells like lavender, the remnants of apple cake, and the scent of scentless laundry detergent. Like my parents' house.

Across the driveway I head into the barn. I know they're starting springtime projects, there's been talk of expanding gardens and trellises and ordering more seeds. It takes a moment for my eyes to adjust to the darkness of the barn. It's a large building that can fit three cars, the tractor, and the buggy with room to spare. Once I can see, it's clear that there's a car missing, part of the mystery solved.

I walk home, empty handed. Winter clearly behind me.

Later in the day I get a text from my mother:

"Sorry we missed you! What an unceremonious end of a perfect reign."

There's been jokes about not letting me win next year, as I ushered in a winter full of snow with my prediction. There's some truth to that. We started with a storm, and ended with a storm, but there was nearly a month where the snow didn't accumulate, and we were worried we wouldn't have a winter wonderland in our backyard. We needn't put our energies into such thoughts.

The words and pages I write each morning start to amass into a beautiful amalgamation of ink and paper, showing where my mind is at, where its spirals take me, how it rights itself, and then wanders into the depths of subjects I didn't realize were just beneath the surface. It's a practice, one that seems obvious or superfluous in the beginning, but as the weeks go by the purpose becomes more and more clear: the practice serves in uncovering myself.

What I'm hearing myself say in the pages is that I am the one holding myself back. Over and over again. I'm the one making choices that lead me to discard entire drafts of novels when the revisions get hard. I'm the one layering sadness over anxiety when I don't get the outcome I'm looking for when I don't change the way I'm doing things.

When I stepped back from my fiction writing I told myself I needed a break, and I did, but how do you know when the break is enough? When does taking a break turn into throwing in the towel? There's a fine line between rest and giving up. For someone like myself, I tip toe over that line and back so often I've gotten used to the view and calling it home so much that the lands of possibilities and dreams feel like a vacation home - someplace to visit but not settle down.

The same goes for living here. After having moved around so much through my formative years, then doing the same as a young adult before eventually settling down in a rental for ten years fully knowing it wasn't permanent, shifting to a space where this is it - this is home for the long run, has not been easy. I'm only now starting to recognize that feeling of disbelief when I let my thoughts wander to a decade or two down the road, it's hard enough to fathom where we are now.

Sometimes when I take Darcey out for walks the time is spent deep in thought. Others it's spent noticing the landscape, the changes in the trees, the way the mud squishes beneath my boots. And then there's times when my mind can't stop thinking about the to do's on my list, the worries of the day, the problems that won't go away. The spiral of thoughts doesn't dissipate, and I find myself regretting the choice to not connect with myself, Darcey, or nature. I've chosen to connect with the things that are out of my control.

The pages written each morning are helping me to choose connection more readily, to notice when I'm veering towards a worry spiral, to be more mindful of the moments that add up to my life. I find the benefits of meditative morning writing spill out through the rest of the day. I smile easier when I hear the birdsong in the woods. I'm present for our walks in a way that allows for constant communication between me and Darcey as she learns how off leash walks work. I'm not judging the moment my mind wanders out the window, through the fields, and down the river. And I'm able to notice when a shift in routine is needed. I get up when my body aches for movement, and sit in stillness when it calls.

Just days after the Vernal Equinox both Fynn and I are sniffling at various points in the day. There's still heaps of snow on the ground, and yet the springtime allergies are afoot. There are reports that the allergy seasons are growing longer as our climate changes, and so once again there's snow in the forecast for the weekend and we're popping allergy tablets, remembering how a few years ago allergy season coincided with our first year of Covid. Though we were isolating we worried each and every day that our allergies were the dreaded virus. Looking back it's hard to put into words the fear that came from simply grabbing our mail, or handling delivered groceries.

For decades when a certain smell hit the air, the scent of springtime, the first wave of warmth to smell like a combination of pollen, mud, and melted snow, it made me think of my Freshman dorm at the University of New Hampshire. Specifically the end of semester celebrations after finals, standing in the back of the dorm with friends as a band played and a cookout ensued, grills manned by resident advisors who were filled with just as many mixed feelings as the rest of us - the exhilaration of finishing a massive load of work and the strong sense of not wanting to leave the world you created in less than a years time.

Now, the smell of spring brings me back to March of 2020 and the season of isolation and endless unknowns. A seemingly new world was created out of necessity in a matter of days, completely out of our control and past the limit of comprehension.

Three years later, remnants of that world surround us. Masks stuffed into pocket books, occasionally found in the dryer. Hand sanitizer at most store entrances. Symptom checks at the doctors office. A second thought when shaking hands. Sleepless nights over cold symptoms. A feeling of being on our own amid a global pandemic. A growing distrust of our leaders, skepticism over restrictions and regulations that feel either too little too late or overreach, depending on your beliefs. Wading tentatively into conversations. Figuring out the balance of wanting a constant personal bubble and a need to connect and live outside of self imposed boundaries.

I remember being so thankful that we had older kids in the early days of the pandemic, that we could explain the protocols and restrictions, the reasons our lives changed so much in such a small time. But as the years go on, and we see the toll it all took, I wish I could go back and protect them more.

When we were on the cusp of locking down I went to Market Basket just to grab a few things. I remember laughing with a woman in the paper goods aisle over the lack of toilet paper, and I remember overhearing a woman on her phone in the toiletries aisle, her cart was stacked high with every over the counter medicine she could grab. She was half whispering, half panicked.

"I don't know," she said into her phone, "but he's saying to stock up, says it's worse than what we're hearing on television." she paused to throw more Pepto Bismol into the cart. "Two weeks? No, he said more like two months at the least."

I remember rolling my eyes, but also my stomach bottoming out, thinking it wouldn't come to that, would it? Three years later we're in a new state, a different landscape, and I wonder if we would have opted for a place of such seclusion if we hadn't endured that time period.

My parents have always been prepared for disasters. When I was still living with them they were always prepared for hurricanes and nor'easters in New Hampshire, and then even more so when they lived in Florida. During the early pandemic days they lived in Pennsylvania, while we were in Massachusetts. Prior to 2020 we were visiting their home and I noticed their stockpiles in the basement, how they would never run out of toilet paper, paper towels, and canned goods - their Costco membership kept them piled high with dry goods.

At some point in the spring of 2020, while on the phone with my mother I mentioned we'd have to start getting creative, as we didn't have a bulk supply of toilet paper. It was an off handed comment, but the following week a gigantic package arrived on our doorstep. It was full of toilet paper. It made me laugh, and then double over with an ache so fierce it left me in tears.

Fast forward to when we were starting to discuss the idea of multi-generational living, and the point came up that if something like that happened again, we'd be able to form a bubble together, help one another out. The impact that deep ache of missing each other was left unsaid, but impacted our decision making more than anyone would admit.

At the end of the month there's a sunny afternoon. After I've finished the errands of the day - dropping one kid off at the dress rehearsal for an upcoming play, a virtual orthodontist appointment for another, cleaning the kitchen and vacuuming the floors, dealing with countless emails and household admin that never seems to end - I slip my laptop and a few books into my bag and make my way out to the cabin. I wave at my parents house as I walk by, not sure if they'll see or not, but it's a habit we've gotten into over the last year and a half. The sun is so bright that there's been noticeable snow melt from earlier in the day when I took Darcey out for a walk. Muddy paths make up more ground cover than snow in spots. My jacket is unzipped, my hair blows in the gentle breeze without cover, and even with my sunglasses I have to squint as the sun is so bright.

Once I get to the clearing where the cabin sits, the wind stills, and I let out an audible sigh. The warmth of the sunshine mixed with the peace of being alone - really alone - feels foreign and yet so right. It's like a puzzle piece sliding into its rightful place, the bumps and edges smooth when you run your fingers over top the whole.

The cabin smells the same all year round, like wood and a little bit of dust and a room that's been closed up through warm days when the windows should be open. I can hear the faint buzz of a fly trying to escape through closed windows, tiny thuds as it butts up against the windowpane. The sound of the clock ticking permeates the one room cabin.

I prop my laptop up on an extended window ledge and bring over a chair. The space overlooks Lower Field, and through the still thin trees I can make out the river. It's no longer snow covered, or even ice covered, and the sun sparkles as the river flows. Along the close edge of the field there's a flock of turkeys grazing on soggy hay where the morning and afternoon sun is relentless. They peck right along the line where the hay meets the snow, I imagine their feet sinking ever so slightly into the mud, down to where the ground is still solid with the remnants of winter. My gaze drifts off, and when I look back at the turkeys, all eight of them are crossing the field, their dark bodies stark against the snow covered field. The birds spread out, some stop and drink from a puddle, others explore, and while they're never out of shouting distance from one another, they each go their own way with the same end point in their sights. Eventually they meander back to the woods, where they make their home.

Writing in the afternoon isn't something I normally do. I've been writing each morning for the last few months, and find that I spend my afternoons on things that don't fill my creative well. Not all the time, but a good number of days I spend the hours in the afternoon waiting on things: to make dinner, to pick up a kid from an activity, to drop off another, for someone to need me. When there's an hour here or there for me to spend as I wish, I don't quite know what to do with myself. In my mind, I've already done my writing for the day, I've checked that box, what's next?

Through my morning pages I've discovered that I long to bring more flow to my days, and I have a desire to feel more ease between activities, to flow from one to the next while touching base with myself, to make choices that are aligned with not only what I want to be doing, but what I want my life to feel like. To feel out my days, not to be ruled by unchecked boxes.

When my children were little there were tiny bursts of time that I made use of in creative ways. I wrote dozens of words in five minute increments, I read countless books one page at a time, I picked up hobbies, retaught myself to knit, dabbled in watercolor. I was inspired. Now, with undoubtedly more time on my hands for myself as my children are more independent and I have bigger blocks of time I can claim as my own, I find myself claiming very little.

And so this time spent at the cabin, in the few hours

before I'm needed to pick someone up from rehearsal, is an example of how I am claiming my time in a more expansive way. I want my writing life to extend far beyond a box to check off, I want my creative life to flow alongside me throughout the day, just as the waters edge ebbs and flows alongside the shore - and maybe as the mud and snow ebb and flow along the field's edge during this transition time of spring. Tomorrow the edge may go one way or the other, depending on the weather. There's snow in the forecast for the weekend, and the temperatures may very well turn the mud to ice by tomorrow morning.

For now, all that I know is that the silence of the cabin is broken by the sound of my fingers on the keyboard, and it sounds like a symphony I've long waited to enjoy. It isn't something that can be shortened to fit on a to-do list, it is far too expressive to check off the list as if it's complete.

The words never end. The creative well never runs dry. They shift with the seasons within, but they are always present.

April

April begins with gusty winds and blooming crocuses. Brilliant purple petals hold tight through the early morning, but by midday, they release their orange center from their clutches, and it feels like spring has sprung.

The mountains of snow are slowly receding, and as we walk the property more often than not we're walking not on snow, but on the still-firm ground left in its muddy wake. The allergies that reared their head briefly last month return, and I still can't help but think they have no right to be here while there's still snow on the ground. Of course, that's not how it works, and the very things that bring delight on our walks - the new buds on trees, blooms near the ground - are what cause some of our noses to run and fullness in our ears.

Early in the month, we find our first tick of the season. I'm sitting on the couch when I feel something crawling on the back of my hand. It's a nymph, just small enough to be noticed but large enough to wreck a body if it's carrying one of many tick-borne illnesses that have been found across the country, notably in our area of Maine. Years ago the kids and I all had Lyme Disease and thankfully were treated with antibiotics that wiped it out of our systems. Ever since, we've been hyper-vigilant regarding tick checks. When Darcey came home with us from the shelter in October of 2021, we got a crash course in finding ticks on a black dog and needing to be even more vigilant. At one of her first checkups, Darcey's labs were positive for Lyme, just weeks after being on our property. Now we do the best we can, but it's always at the back of my mind when the temperatures rise above freezing.

Three seasons of the year our fields are full of tall grasses and hay, prime breeding grounds for the tiny arachnids, but we've also seen them right outside our doors, making even taking the dog outside for a quick walk around the house an event when we come inside. We give her a good once over with a brush, and then run our hands over her trying to feel for smooth bumps that could jump from her to the floor or us.

Just at the very moment we start to feel relief from the depths of winter with sunshine and warmer temps, we're reminded of the dangers right outside our door. In winter time the dangers are cold and ice, the rest of the year they're ticks. It sounds dramatic to be as concerned with tiny things as we are, but I can still feel the way my neck stiffened as the disease spread through me, what it was like when the bullseye rash appeared, and how long it took me to recover not only from Lyme but from the treatment of antibiotics.

And so April starts off with a sobering reminder of the realities of living next to and within the wilderness. Of course, we have concerns about bigger animals: predators, rabid creatures, fisher cats, bears, and even the hawks with large wingspans can send shivers down my spine when I'm walking alone and see one hovering above me. But all of those we can see, sometimes hearing them prior to visibility. The scary part about ticks and tick bites is they're easily missed. The landscape of my own body is covered with freckles and moles, which look similar to an embedded tick unless you look closely. The season of doing double takes in the mirror before jumping in the shower is upon us.

Early last spring Lucas and I went for a drive down the coast, and on the way back I scratched at an itch just beneath my hairline on the back of my neck. My fingers grazed a bump, and I asked Lucas the question we are all too familiar with, "tick or mole?" It wasn't a mole. We stopped at the first drugstore we could find for a pair of tweezers as our tick remover was left at home.

It's a constant conversation, a constant threat, and a constant possibility even on days we don't leave the house.

At times I know it has affected all of our willingness to get outside and enjoy the outdoors. From now until the dry heat of August comes we will cover ourselves in repellent, tall socks and boots, and still be careful where we walk. I'll double check the sheets before climbing into bed. None of us like to live in a place of fear, but I'd be lying if I said it didn't impact us, the kids especially. They came of age with me yelling, "Tick checks!" whenever we came inside from a hike or even playing in the backyard of our previous home. While it was a regular occurrence, I know it was also something that at times felt invasive and unwelcome to kids with sensory issues, and the human want and need for agency.

Trust issues come to play in this. Trusting ourselves, but being aware and knowledgeable, maybe having too much knowledge.

The wind is relentless. Even after only two days, it feels like the wind just won't quit. The temperatures are springlike, meaning above freezing, but unless you're curled up in a sunbeam there's a chill that lingers. On the first Friday of the month, I start a fire in the afternoon so the house will be toasty when my parents come over for dinner. I put the logs in the fireplace, and as it grows I warm myself and watch the flames dance.

I turn the oven on and start chopping vegetables for dinner. There's music streaming through the speakers, and my hips sway as I peel sweet potatoes. Between the fireplace, the stove, and dancing, I'm warmer than I have been in days.

When I think about spring, the one thought that comes to mind after allergies is being cold. Growing up in New England you'd think that I would remember spring does not equate to warmer temperatures. And yet, as soon

as the sun is around more, there's the desire to shed layers.
There's a bit of wishful thinking that if we think warm
thoughts if we dress for the weather like we're supposed to
dress for the job we want, we'll manifest tee shirt weather.

Over dinner, we start talking about renaming some
of the landmarks on the property. There's little about this
property that doesn't feel like ours anymore, but the names
the previous owners gave for certain places have stuck. The
House Site is a clearing where at one point they were going
to build another house, and the name has stuck. But there's
a desire to rename what is ours. For some on the property,
even the name our private street was given is a source
of discontent, but the process and red tape surrounding
renaming a street has helped the given name survive.

"What about Hobbit Hill?" suggests my mother.

There's no objection, and so from this day forward,
we start to use the new name, Hobbit Hill, instead of The
House Site. Other names surface, Chickadee Lane and
Cabin Way, but nothing is set in stone. Part of the problem
is no one knows what area the others are referring to,
perhaps this is when a name matters. Perhaps this is when
it's necessary for something to be named instead of just left
to exist. Giving names to wild areas that we've tamed for
our use takes it one more step away from the wilderness,

which leaves me feeling conflicted. Yes, it's helpful to know where we're talking about, to have landmarks. But will we still be able to get lost within them after we've claimed them and made them more human?

The second week of April brings a change in weather patterns. The temperatures start off in the 60s, and end in the 70s with a myriad of numbers in between. Easter Sunday is full of sunshine and ham, deviled eggs and blue sky, brilliant purple crocuses and jelly beans. After lunch, we play croquet in the yard behind my parent's house where the sun hits for most of the day and the snow has been gone for enough time that the ground is dry. There are only five mallets and so I sit the games out, choosing instead to relax on a sun-blanketed rock with Darcey at my side. We watch half-heartedly, otherwise occupied with the receding snow lines in the space between our houses and the cabin, the woods. Dad is the first one out of the game, and he meanders over and sits on the ground, leaning up against the rock beside me. There's an ease between us, one that wasn't there a few years ago, one that has surprised us both since becoming neighbors.

Amid quiet conversation, Dad looks down and spots a tick on his sweatshirt. I remove it for him as it's just beyond his reach, and then we're both up on our feet and decide to wander across the yard to the wildflower meadow and the lavender patch, and eventually up to a crab apple tree that was transplanted last year from a crowded area to an open one for visual appeal. It was an experiment, as most things are here on our homestead, and we've all been waiting to see if it made it through the winter.

Much to our delight, there's a sprig of new growth and buds on the branches. Maybe this experiment has legs after all.

Monday comes and with it even more snow melts. On our morning walk we don't even put on hats, and gloves stay behind in the basket of winter accessories. Later in the day, we're inside and hear the sound of the buggy for the first time this spring. It's a four-wheeler with a rollover cage that was the previous owner's, but we acquired it for a steal in the exchange of property.

Darcey's ears perk up, and she lets out a little bark to tell us she hears it, too. By the end of last fall, the noise barely registered for her, but now it's novel once again.

I smile to myself, knowing what that means: that Dad is out there cleaning up piles of brush and debris leftover from winter storms, something he's been anxious to start. He's found a solid enough path down to the brush pile along the edge of Lower Field, and he's started on his mental list of to-do's he's been adding to all winter long.

After dinner, we take a walk along our usual route. As we head from Hobbit Hill down to Upper Field there are still areas of deep snow. Down near the bottom where for months there's been only our footprints now lay tire tracks from where Dad must have made an attempt to come through, but the snow and soft ground were too much for the buggy. All along the trail are now muddy rivets made from tires, over and through piles of snow.

Once again conflicting thoughts arise. There's discomfort in the marks we leave behind on the land and knowledge that the clean-up is necessary in some areas, and we're helping to maintain the forest in parts. Stewards of the land, that's what we strive to be. And yet the tire tracks through the snow remind me of the fine line we dance around.

Writing is like that too - trying to manhandle stories into being. Often writing feels like a dance between the idea and reality of the story, and my job as a writer is to figure out how much of the words need crafting, versus letting them be as they initially formed. It's about deciding what stays, and what is left behind, what can be extracted, and what needs to stay rooted and become more wild. The words are only a small part of writing. For me, it's so much more about how the words feel, both initially and then after tending.

The outdoors beckons with mild temperatures. The kids and I find ourselves at home one afternoon thanks to a cancellation, and I ask the question that has a 50/50 chance of getting a yes: does anyone want to go exploring? To my delight and surprise, they both say yes and before long we're outside just the three of us, like when they were younger.

Before living here, we'd only lived in small spaces, indoors and out, apartments at first and then the half a duplex we inhabited for the last ten years. When we reminisce about the old place and I ask what their favorite memories entail, both kids have favorite climbing trees they talk about, one being a dogwood that had to be removed thanks to strong roots making their way into the pipes. Now, with an abundance of trees at their fingertips, it's more likely that each of the kids spends their time in their rooms. It's the season they're in, one that doesn't always align with the seasons the rest of us are experiencing.

But today, they are along for the adventure in body if not entirely in spirit. While it's warm, it's also overcast. We're dressed in various iterations of spring fashion: Paige has on overall shorts with a tee shirt, crocheted sweater, and sneakers; Fynn is in jeans, a corduroy jacket, and his tall muck boots; I'm wearing a short sleeve hand knit sweater over a linen top and I've shelved my winter boots in favor of green wellies. We're a bit of a motley crew as we depart, walking past my parent's house and up through the woods by the cabin, down Sledding Hill, and into Lower Field where we take a left and walk along the tree line until we see water on the left, a clear sign of the swamp. A hawk departs from a tree and swoops from one side of the field to the other.

The field isn't a flat area of ground, it undulates with tiny hills and valleys that you feel most when cross-country skiing. It's hard to see the swells of ground when you're looking at a mass of green hay, or football fields of white snow, but they create mini ponds that drain either off to the river or down into the swamp.

The last time we explored the swamp was at least a year ago. It was a day similar to this, where some wore short sleeves while the snow lingered. Today, across the field towards the riverside where the sun hits the least amount of time, the snow still covers a good bit of ground.

The same goes for the swamp, only ice instead of snow. Because of the tree cover, barely any snow made it to the ground, but the pools of water are still half frozen. It'll take multiple days of the weather we're having - highs in the 60s - to defrost all the nooks and crannies here. We keep an eye out for animals, but only through the trees that divide the wetland area and the field do we see robins landing in the big open area. As we walk our feet crunch the leaves that are strewn across the solid ground we at times have to hop to in order to not end up in shin-deep water or even deeper in mud and muck.

Downed trees are returning to the earth, and tree stumps are taken over by mushrooms and moss. The swamp is one area of our property that has been and will remain, untouched by farm equipment.

It takes a while for the kids to get lost in the outdoors, but slowly it happens. If I watch carefully, but not too closely, I can see the rigidity of their movements melt from controlled steps to graceful leaps across the water. We each go our own way, and when I turn around I see they're both up trees and my heart soars. This is why I ask, even if half the time they say no. I hear wobbly laughter as one balances while walking across a downed tree that hangs in another, and no sooner are there footsteps not walking, but running across the decaying leaves to see what the other is up to.

They spend the next bit of time exploring together, testing limits and boundaries between them and the natural world with balance, skill, and the occasional wobble. I join them here and there, showing them I can still balance on moss-covered logs to cross a moat-type area, soaking it all up. The fresh air, their presence, the moment. This is the season of parenting I'm in, facilitating and being present, offering options and security while they find their way in the world.

While we're enveloped in our surroundings, the outside world is never far. When standing anywhere on the property you can still hear the hum of traffic thanks to a main road by the house and another that sits parallel to the edge of Lower Field. If you follow the river to the west it meanders and goes under a bridge that holds the largely traveled Route 4. We could canoe our way down to the grocery store but have yet to do so.

Maybe that's why our acreage feels so special. We know there are paths to civilization, and yet there are also paths to untouched areas like the swamp. Just a ten-minute walk from the house and we're surrounded by trees, moss, water, and earth. Not quite immersed, never out of cell phone range, one foot in and one foot out. Maybe special isn't quite the right word. Sometimes it feels like a time capsule. Private, but not entirely. Wild, but safe. Expansive, but still a little contained. The push and pull of February come to mind, and the contradictions and lines we dance around controlling and maintaining a wild environment, or even the stories I'm writing, feel similar. Inhabiting spaces that are not entirely meant for us, how do we do so while still keeping a sense of reverie, honoring the way it has evolved, with and without our footsteps.

Tonight the wind is fierce. It sounds like a low and sad saxophone and keeps me awake or in fitful dreams of

Lucas saying, "It's okay, we get only one night a month with the wind…" I worry about the small table and set of chairs I set out earlier that day, I can picture them taking flight and ending up smashing the windows of the car sitting in the driveway.

But when I wake, the chairs are right where I left them, the table too. The car is in one piece. We don't find any downed trees on our morning walk. Everything is safe. We are all safe. It was just a wind-fueled night of broken sleep, of a mind running wild with what ifs.

Later that week on the coattails of our swamp adventure I throw out the idea of an adventure to the coast. The winds have died down and the temperature has soared. Last year about the same time we headed towards Phippsburg and Popham Beach, we attempt the same trip. I note with satisfaction that we're finding our own rhythm of activities and adventures, repeating what served us last year.

It's still off-season, and while the parking lot is more crowded than the last few times we've come, it's hardly busy. What I love about early spring trips to the beach on gorgeous days is that everyone you encounter is in a good mood. There's something about the first time your bare feet sink into the sand in early spring, you can't help but smile. There's a mix of ages visiting the beach - retirees, mothers with small children, a group of high school kids from a non-traditional school, couples, and people who look like they're on their lunch break. At first glance, you would think that age is the deciding factor for how many or few clothes people wear on any given April beach day, but it makes little difference. There are teens huddled under blankets with hoodies on as well as some in swim trunks, there are people my age with winter jackets, as well as toddlers with woolens. And then there's a plethora of rain boots, bare feet, and winter white arms gracing our presence, on all ages.

We set down a blanket and a beach bag, the kids take off their shoes and head off for a walk while I sit with a book.

I don't know if it's the salt air, the sand, or what, but I've always felt more myself at the shoreline. As I kick my sandals off and strip layers, I feel at ease in my movements. There's a flow that happens here, one that leaves me feeling, for lack of better words, sexy. The sand slows movements, my hips sway more when I walk, and when I lay down on the beach blanket I can feel the sand shift under me, hugging my curves and simply holding me.

I've felt that same grounding, the same of the earth feeling when camping. Coming home with campfire clinging to my hair and body feels the same way as when I come home from the beach with salt clinging to my hair and skin. Those earthy smells cling and act as perfume, reminding me I'm from this earth, this ground. I'm not separate.

The kids spend nearly an hour exploring. At various points, I look up from my book and can't spot them. The lines of the beach curve around sand dunes and protected areas. In my mind, I can picture them on the other side of the bend, where the water is shallow and the banks of sand steep. Paige is more than likely in the water, Fynn standing by with his hands in his pockets, keeping watch with that smile he has reserved only for his sister.

I turn back to my book and spend the next moments alternately reading and closing my eyes to soak in as much of the sun as I can, listening to the waves and the wind. Before I know it there are two shadows across the blanket, the kids have returned. Paige's shorts are wet, and her legs look frozen, but there's a smile strewn across her face. Fynn's pant legs are rolled up and dry as a bone. He gives me a lopsided smile as he settles down on the blanket. They regale me with tales of what they saw, the people who called out to ask Paige how the water felt, the seashells they collected. None of which is unlike any other spring beach trip we've taken over the years. There is comfort in the things that remain unchanged, no matter what state or town you reside in.

Our time at the coast lasts long enough for us to take the essence of the day home with us, our hearts and spirits lighter, our smiles wider. We'll need the memory of sunshine and salt air to get us through the remainder of spring.

Maine is a large state compared to others I've lived in. Its thirty five thousand square miles is three times the size of Massachusetts. There are jokes about people who have spent a lifetime in Maine and haven't left the state. The state, much like many others, has everything you could need, even geographically. Mountains, the ocean, lakes, we even have a desert. And in the span of one week, I hit them all, desert aside.

A few days after our trip to the coast, my father and

I head deep into the state to find the Davistown Museum in Liberty. For Christmas, I gifted my father a book on ancient tools and promised a trip to the museum. It's a small place with tools, art, and local history. They also have another location in Hulls Cove, in Acadia National Park. On this beautiful spring day when the fields are just wet enough to still hinder the work with the tractor, Dad cashes in on his gift.

Liberty is a small town much like our own, and in these few weeks when the snow is gone, leaving behind any dirt and grime that it held in its banks, the daffodils play a key role in reminding us there's so much beauty right around the corner. There are patches of greening yards, but without the daffodils and crocuses, the landscape here and at home would look dull and drab.

We park at the town hall and walk up a hill to the downtown area which consists of a few storefronts: a flower shop, a graphic arts store filled with tee shirts and other printed items as well as cold beverages, and a tool store across the street from the museum.

The museum itself takes up the second and third floors atop the graphic arts store. The stairway is narrow and steep, and the museum area on both floors is chock-full of artifacts. The rooms are steeped in history. There are Native American artifacts from the Maliseet, Micmac, Passamaquoddy, and Penobscot tribes. Collectively they are called the Wabanaki, People of the Dawnland. And then there are blacksmithing tools, hundreds of year-old cooper tools, delicate jewelry-making instruments, whaling apparatus, axes of all shapes and sizes, hand planes plenty, as well as sculptures made out of tools that leave you with a question of which pieces are art and which are tools, or are they all one and the same?

The attendant pops in at one point, but otherwise, we have the place to ourselves. There's literature throughout the museum, some special documents, and write-ups about the acquisition of various tools. It's similar to my experience overall in Maine, the information is there for you if you want it, but there is no one to hold your hand through whatever process you're going through, be it finding out about the providence of the whale harpoon in a museum, or figuring out how to get your driver's license or register your car. While people are glad to help, even going out of their way to extend kindness, there's a general feeling that coddling isn't a thing here. It's a no-nonsense way of being.

The museum is hands-on, and anything that isn't ensconced in a glass case is available to touch and hold.

Dad shows me how the palm-sized planers work with the blade on the bottom, and how to adjust the thickness. I touch my finger to it gently, it's barely there but sharp and would make an impact on a piece of wood let alone my finger tip.

We linger over craftsmanship, Dad mentions a display he thinks Toby, a printmaker, might enjoy seeing. We talk about the physicality of the tools, the heaviness. Over by the axes Dad picks up one and gives a low whistle, hands it to me with his eyebrows raised so I know its heft.

"Makes you appreciate the chainsaw, doesn't it?" I say. He nods.

The amount of creativity in the museum astounds me. The ingenuity, and the way people have used tools to make work a little bit easier. I think about one of my favorite knitwear designers, and how she says if you have an issue getting the right gauge try and change your tools instead of the way your body works. The adage of working smarter, not harder, comes to mind.

We stay long enough to take multiple laps around the museum and dozens of photos to share with the rest of the family. I sign the guest book and drop a few dollars into the donation box before we walk down the creaky stairs towards the front porch where we find a mother and

105

daughter sitting at a rustic table having their lunch. The mother is listening with full attention as her preteen talks animatedly, there are two glass soda bottles in front of them, straws sticking out the tops. It's a sweet scene, and I smile as we walk by.

At the car, I start unpacking our tailgating lunch. I hand Dad the container I packed for him and then open my own. We're both sitting in the back end of my Subaru, feet hanging down. Dad tells me a story about their old neighbors, the ones they lived by before moving next door to us. We're staring at Liberty's town hall, noting the differences between it and our own. The conversation is easy and simple. In order to live next door to one another we made clear boundaries early on about what we could absolutely not talk about: politics. On the drive neither of us mentions political signs we see, instead, we opt for topics like the landscape, the budding trees, the flowers, and yes, the weather. But even without mentioning the elephant or donkey in the room, over the last few years we've realized that beyond politics our values are similar if not the same in most areas. It's been a reminder to me, and I hope to both of us, that politics isn't the end all be all. How you care about your neighbors, your friends, your family, and humanity, that's where you see the truth in your heart. The stuff that comes out of our mouths isn't nearly as important as the actions we take on a daily basis that show how we move through the world.

As we sit and enjoy our lunch I notice an older couple who drove and parked near us, they're now walking by the front of our car, but I turn just in time to notice them look our way, and then smile a smile that expresses the way I felt walking by the mother and daughter just a few moments earlier. With Dad telling a story about new neighbors down the road from us, I grin into my sandwich and then close my eyes for a second, taking in everything about this moment.

The next day we're at home for a Sunday of zero obligations. The weather forecast had predicted an overcast day, and some rain late. Instead, the sun shines brightly and the temperatures are warm.

We take Darcey for a walk, and the conversation turns to the future, the way way future. Yesterday Dad asked me if we'd thought about what we'll do after he and Mom are gone, did we have any thoughts or plans? I told him that we had gotten so far as thinking we want to make sure our kids have the choice of staying here and taking on the land. If they're not interested, well, we hadn't gotten that far. We don't know what life will hold for us.

I bring this up with Lucas, and he mentions a conversation he had with a coworker the last time he was in the city for work. His colleague asked if Lucas just liked it up here, or loved it. Standing now in Lower Field, in the vast open space where everything we can see is ours. He shares that he said what he loves is the quiet. The peacefulness.

I feel the same way.

At first, we were overwhelmed simply to have our own home, something we'd worked towards for years. And it's only now, nearly two years into living here, that we're fully grasping what we have, and what a responsibility it is to care for this land.

Later in the morning, Lucas wants to tackle a pile of wood from storm damage that's been cut into logs but needs splitting, so we get set up by the woodshed next to the house. The electric log splitter does the trick, but it's a slow and steady job. By the time Paige and I get outside to help Lucas, he already has a pile of split logs ready to stack. He and the kids did a good deal of work outside when Dad and I were off the day before, and so when we walk outside, Lucas looks surprised and pleased that Paige is with me. He asks if she wants to do the splitting, and she says sure and jumps right in, leaving the stacking to me. Darcey wanders over to my parent's porch where it's shady and watches us from afar.

All winter long we've wondered how to get the kids out of their rooms more, and here we are a few weeks into spring and it seems we were fighting their and our natural tendencies to stay cozy and warm. Now that the weather is mild, they both head out for walks on their own or together, and they're both willing to help with the outdoor work. We often lament that if we had moved here five or ten years ago, the kids would have had a different, deeper connection to this place. For us, it's easy to see the small amount of time they have left before leaving the nest, but for them, maybe it's enough to tuck into a day's work driving the buggy to and from the brush pile, splitting logs with their father, laughing over how the wood splits into wonky shapes, seeing how a downed tree becomes fuel for the fire in a few years time.

Maybe our timing is just what it needs to be. Maybe we needn't worry over kids spending winter in their bedrooms, warm and safe, and them not having the connection to this place we think they should. Maybe the one they have is exactly what they need, and it will grow as they do, mature, and age over time as nature intends.

By the end of the month, we're full of April showers, with cloudy days stretching from one to another. Not only does the rain enhance the green grass that's filling in around the property, but it also showcases the growing buds on the trees. There's green everywhere we look, with splashes of red around the maples. The forsythia bush behind the house has started flowering, a dash of yellow flashes next to the brown of the house siding. Closer to the ground I can see where the hydrangeas I planted last Mother's Day are coming up through the mulch, unfurling the more they reach for the sun.

On the third cloudy day in a row, the chill finally reaches my bones. Lucas just cleaned the fireplace, wiped down the glass window, and emptied some of the ashes. In my mind that signaled the end of use until autumn, but today's weather challenges that idea. I stack a few logs and mix in some kindling, get the fire going and sit down on the couch with my knitting. I'm on the second sleeve of a sweater for Adrienne, my sister-in-law. It's the final part before I weave in the ends. While they were visiting she asked if I'd knit her a sweater, and we worked together to choose a design, the yarn, and the colors. It's a yoked sweater with a color work design on the yolk as well as the bottom of the sleeves. She chose a blue-gray for the main color and a fiery yellow-orange for the contrast. Watching the flames through the pristine glass of the stove, it's hard to miss the similarities between the fire and the sweater at hand. Charcoal and yellows, oranges and gray, they dance together in a way that looks animated and comfortably fierce, a mesmerizing combination. The thing about fires during this season is that you never know when the last of the season will be, much like the last time you reach for a heavy woolen sweater.

At night I fall asleep to the sound of peepers along with the comforting knowledge that while there are many lasts upon us, there are also many firsts right around the corner, and the return of snowbanks and cozy nights curled up by the fire will return in due time.

May

April's showers bleed over into May. The first of the month falls on a Monday, and while I'm on my first cup of tea Lucas rushes around inside and out. Out the window I can see him lugging the rain barrel that wintered in the barn to its three season home in the yard to catch run off from our roof.

"There's water in the basement," he offers as an explanation, as if one was needed besides the rain that's been coming down in buckets. There's no urgency in his voice, but his actions have the telltale signs of a Monday morning: the door slams just a little bit, curse words linger under his breath, the palpable feeling of not having enough time.

Before long he's at his desk, and I'm still tucked into my tea with journal pages in front of me. I've written three lines, but between them all, I've chatted with the dog, responded to a few texts, and said good morning to the kids. And I wonder why I haven't made any headway on this morning practice recently.

I write down that I haven't been protecting my time. My space. My writing. In my attempt to flow and have writing be a part of my day in an organic way, I haven't given it the room it deserves. I'm still expecting it to magically take up space on its own, to fit in amongst the errands and daily jobs.

While I believe that writing looks like life, it still needs to be protected.

Later on, it's still raining, but I want to be the person who willingly goes out for walks in the rain, so I do. Darcey and I take the long way and walk from Hobbit Hill to Upper Field, and then down the incline that's been rendered muddy and slippery to Lower Field. I watch my steps carefully. Puddles form where the hill meets the field. I'm in my rain boots so I take the opportunity to puddle jump like my kids did when they were little. Darcey watches from a distance with cautious eyes. I jump a few more times and then with a lingering smile on my lips we head into the woods to the Bucket Trail.

It rained 3 inches overnight, and it's still falling. Now where there's normally a multiple-foot drop to the river, there's water at the edge of the trail, and in low spots it's made its way across the path in little streams. We forge on, Darcey sniffs every lichen-covered tree while I notice the water droplets on the trees, how they cling to the pine needles.

I may be wearing boots and covered in rain gear, but it makes me think of how I felt at the coast last month when I went barefoot in the sand and felt the sway of my hips. I look up through the trees and feel what must be the effects of forest bathing: calm.

I can hear and see the river rushing by, and after we walk as far as our property goes we turn around. By the time we're back in the field, there's more mud and puddles against the backdrop of green grass and hay.

Back at home with my body warmed up thanks to the puddle jumping and walking I head to the basement for a workout. Half an hour later I'm high on endorphins, and when I walk back towards the stairs I see the water Lucas was talking about. Knowing he has meetings for the rest of the day, and still feeling energetic, I grab the wet vac and start suctioning up puddles of water. Dealing with the basement has been on our list of to-do's since we moved in, but as it's not an every-storm kind of issue… it's gotten pushed to the side again and again.

There's something satisfying about using the wet vac, seeing the progress you're making and hearing the water slosh in the container. But it's cumbersome work, the hose isn't incredibly flexible, and at one point I have to readjust, and while twisting the hose I stand up quickly with all the force one would jump up with during an exercise video, and smack my head straight into the only overhead pvc pipe I could possibly hit throughout the entire basement.

I let out a string of expletives and hold the spot on my head where the pain shoots. Stars swim into view, I close my eyes but they're still dancing in front of me. The pain is deep and it lingers, my mood changes instantly from invigorated to plain old pissed off. I finish cleaning up the water on the section of floor in front of me, and then coil up the various parts of the machine and walk slowly upstairs.

By the time I finish taking a shower and making

something to eat for lunch, it becomes harder and harder
to keep my eyes open. I feel wobbly when I get up from
my perch at the kitchen counter and make my way into the
office to tell Lucas something isn't right, and I'm scared.

Not even an hour later the two of us are sitting
in the Emergency Room of Saint Mary's Hospital in
Lewiston. We wait for three hours, Lucas only leaves
my side to grab us bottles of water and a snack from the
vending machine. We listen as symptoms of other patients
unfold, coughs from one corner, vomiting in another, slow
steps of others as they walk by holding themselves only as
one does when in pain. I sit there, willing my head to stop
aching so we can leave, worrying I'll be told I disrupted our
entire day and waited this long for a simple bump on the
head.

Eventually, my name is called, and they ask if
I need a wheelchair, but I decline. Halfway down the
hallway, trying to follow an expedient nurse, I regret the
decision. She apologizes that there isn't a room, and she
settles me into a makeshift area with a gurney and privacy
panels.

A few moments later the doctor comes in, apologizing for the wait and the accommodations. There's a Mickey Mouse figurine attached to his stethoscope, and for the first time in my short history of emergency room visits it strikes me as funny that this man is probably my age, if not Lucas'. He asks what happened, and I explain, giving all the details.

"And did you finish vacuuming after you hit your head?" he asks, a twinkle in his eye.

I shrug my shoulders and say yes, of course.

Beside me, I hear Lucas give a nervous laugh and know he's shaking his head. The doctor just nods and gets out a flashlight to examine my eyes.

After a few more questions and further examination, he tells me I have a concussion. He says it sounds scary, but because of the symptoms, we shouldn't worry. He says to not concentrate too hard on anything, avoid screens, that light movement like walking could speed up recovery.

He sends us on our way with a prescription for rest and Tylenol. We pay our bill and before long we're outside, the rain from the morning left behind for a beautiful spring day in New England, daffodils and late afternoon sunshine greet us in the courtyard.

There's a feeling of relief, not only that I don't need

to worry about all the places my aching head went - brain bleeds, aneurysms, passing out mid-sentence - but that what I felt was spot on. Something was not right, it wasn't my imagination. After a lifetime of questioning my own body, my own thoughts, learning to trust when it says something isn't right has been a challenge. This time, I listened. And I'm so glad I did.

On our way home I call my father to let him know what transpired at the ER. When he answers he sounds far away and distracted, and it turns out he's out back with the farmer who deals with the hay in our fields. The water crested the river bank and Lower Field flooded. There's no longer a path to the Bucket Trail, or any trail at all. The woods are flooded, it's all underwater, there's fish swimming in our hayfields.

The next day we walk down to see the damage done by the river, the changes, and the effects. Mom and Dad tell us the geese who have made their homes by the river were angry, their nests had been swept away.

The night before, I slept fitfully, still concerned about my poor jostled brain, still full of unknowns over what this injury means for my days. But the fresh air fills my lungs and steadies me as I walk gingerly along the paths I could navigate in my sleep. Lucas stays by my side as we walk, the dog close by as if she knows the changes in my gait mean something is up.

The field is still full of water, but Lucas is able to walk out into the middle, the top of the water doesn't reach the height of his muck boots. Already, the water has started to recede, the four inches of rain in total has done its job. There's talk in town of flooded roads and the repairs needed. The mulch pile Dad and Lucas have worked on with the chipper is surrounded by water, small piles of it now sit washed-up in out of place areas. Lucas is up to nearly the top of his boots in water, the sky is lightening, and we're getting a brief break from the storms. Yesterday afternoon there were blue skies, but another storm is on the brink.

All of the plans for the field, and the farmer's timeline for fertilizing and harvesting, is now changed. He tells us how he was behind already, and thankfully so. He knows of farmers who fertilized the week before, now all of that has been swept away.

The field, the weather, and so much more are out of our hands and control. Accidents, freak of nature events, concussions, these things happen. Instead of fighting them, maybe the only thing we can do is wait for the water to recede and see what's left behind.

The advice everywhere I search is to not concentrate on things for long periods of time and to not use screens. In the first week after the accident, I try to stick to it, though one day I have the television on in the background for something to listen to. The next day my headache is worse, and it feels like a punch to the gut. If I can't use my phone, computer, television, or read, write in a journal, or knit for very long, what am I to do?

There's a lot of staring at the walls, lots of napping. Texts with friends here and there as my head allows. But the days feel fragmented. Some I don't even shower, and I dress in pajamas no matter the hour. Each night I go to bed thinking tomorrow will be better, and for the most part, it is. There's improvement every day. My balance comes back first, and eventually, I start to notice I'm not reaching for the big red bottle of Tylenol nearly as often. Lucas reminds me of what the emergency room doctor said and encourages me to go on walks with him and Darcey. Nothing big, and nothing fast, but I'm still outside and moving. Maybe if I move my body, my head will follow along. Some days it does.

Later in the week I spend time journaling with pen and paper and find myself writing about the choice to be miserable. I feel like I have to act miserable in order to deserve rest, like I can't enjoy the quiet, the space to recover. If it's forced rest we fight it - is that a societal standard? You must not enjoy being bedridden, you must fight to get back on your feet as soon as possible.

But the fighting takes energy. What if we spent that energy instead on gratitude, or if not gratitude, acceptance. Acceptance over what the moment holds, and what is needed. The next moment may require something else, too. Maybe all that being miserable takes up more energy than acceptance.

Our strolls start to give my days structure. Every day that passes my feet feel more grounded on the earth, and as it's a slower pace I feel like I'm on the kind of walks we called noticing walks when the kids were little. Really, they were our regular walks, but I'd encourage them to pay close attention to things they might otherwise pass by, I'd encourage them to notice the world that was at their fingertips and toes.

At first, we're mostly aware of the water - where it has receded and where it lingers. One day we make it back over to the Bucket Trail and find that when the river pulled itself back it left behind traces of its attempt to overtake the land, and the once pine needle-covered trail now looks like a dust storm whipped through covering everything in its wake.

There are puddles in parts of the field, but for all the talk of what debris could be left behind, we don't see anything that doesn't belong -there are no rubber tires, no bits of trash, all the rusty buckets that line the Bucket Trail stayed in place. We've seen garbage floating in the river, but none of it made it into the fields, none of it washed ashore.

We're not the only ones keeping an eye on the fields. My father monitors it daily to see when it's dry enough for the tractor to make its way around the edges to work on projects that are in progress, fallen trees need to be collected, and he's anxious to get the paths cut so we have places to walk once the hay starts growing. Before the flooding, it was almost safe for him to do so, but now, it'll be another few weeks.

The week before Mother's Day, Mom and I go plant nursery hopping. As I'm still not feeling entirely steady, she drives, and we make the same trek we made last year for our first initial exploration. Last year we didn't know what was around us, what nursery to go to for what type of plant. This year we're more familiar with the area, the towns, and roads, the way the river runs alongside us on our travels.

The first nursery we visit is a family-owned and run business called Young's. As soon as we step out of the car we see a few people running across the parking lot and then across the street. There's a blustery May breeze, and dust from the parking area kicks up, through which we watch as half a dozen people try and corral a cow that's gotten loose from its pen. On one side of the road is the farm, and on another an expansive nursery with four high tunnels filled with varieties of flowers, vegetables, succulents, fruit trees, and more. There's also a barn used to store fertilizers, composts, and soil, and another structure that houses the rest of the goods - lawn ornaments and planters and pots, supplies for fairy houses, and bottles of water and local honey.

Mostly, I'm just along for the ride and some inspiration. My mother is the one who knows what she's doing and can hold her own in a conversation with any expert gardener. As we walk from high tunnel to high tunnel, she exclaims with excitement the names of plants, though they sound like a foreign language to my ear, I understand every fourth word or so.

She's also a quilter, and as she walks through rows of flowers plans come together in her head and out loud, it reminds me of the countless trips we've made to fabric stores over the years, how she gathers bolts of fabric, knows just how much to cut, and then pieces the colors and shapes together to create something cohesive and beautiful in a way that's so much more than simply a warm blanket.

We spend a good two hours at Young's and end up having multiple conversations with the owner. When we share that we've seen their ads on YouTube he says that he just does the grunt work, the hands-on labor, it's his kids and grandkids who deal with all the tech stuff, all the marketing. Later on, when we see him a second time, my mom asks if they'll get wiped out over Mother's Day weekend.

"Sure," he says, "but there'll be more later, there's always more coming."

"It's just so early," notes Mom. "It's all gorgeous but it's too early to plant so many things."

He agrees and tells us about having to come outside in the middle of the night to cover some plants they moved outside, to protect them from the frost.

"But people want to plant when they want to plant", he says, "regardless of the frost dates."

After buying two planters full of hardy pansies, we leave with heads full of ideas and drive to the next place. At Gammons, a few towns over, we are met with more large bushes and trees than at Young's, which is what we have our sights set on, namely - rhododendrons. My parents generously offered to buy Lucas and me each a bush, one for Mother's Day and one for Father's Day. A pair, just like us. We find rows and rows of them, of all sizes. We go for medium-sized bushes and look carefully at the tags to ensure matching colors. There are yellows, pinks of various shades, and purples. We pick two in a deep pink that borders on purple, place them on a wagon, and wheel around to look at the rest of the place. Mom's mentioned adding a few apple trees to the yard between our houses, for visual interest and to distract their bedroom view of the side of our garage and the outdoor components of a heat pump, so we wheel around our bushes to the fruit tree section. They're more established than the ones at Young's, and their varieties are more sweeping.

We don't stay for long, as I'm starting to fade, and it's getting close to dinner time. We don't pick up an apple tree, but Mom finds a display of wintergreen plants, and she adds six to our wagon as well as compost for the rhododendrons. We don't visit the third nursery on our list on the way home, but we are content with our purchases, cheeks flushed with sunshine and conversation, minds full of what's to come in our gardens.

On Mother's Day, we plant the rhododendrons. Fynn and Lucas dig the holes while I stand by and supervise, feeling both helpless and grateful. Pollen swirls around us, and Fynn and I are both sniffling by the time we've been outside for not even five minutes. But there's sunshine, and even though the wind is rough with us, it feels good to be outside. They mix soil and compost, and we water the bushes, dreaming of what they'll one day become.

When we first moved in, the gully that sits between our property and the road was filled with tall wildflowers and weeds. Technically the state is in charge of maintaining that space, but take a drive down our road, or any other state road in rural towns, and you'll find them all overgrown with their own kind of beauty. It was an eyesore to my father, and when he first mowed the overgrowth it felt as though we were suddenly on display to passerby-ers, our privacy - though it was minimal - removed. Our house sits just behind the gulley, and the road-facing windows are in the master bedroom and the living room. Most days I leave the bedroom curtains drawn for privacy, but we'd love to have the rooms feel open bright during the day.

We'd talked about different options and different bushes, but ultimately we didn't want to hinder our view from the driveway as we pulled out onto the road. And so maybe the solution was closer to the house, we figured. And in came the thoughts of rhododendrons, which we'd had at our previous house and they served much the same purpose we were looking for here, blocking part of the window, drawing the eye to its purple flowers instead of whatever is happening inside. A buffer. Here, it might be years in the making, but it's a start, an intention, a long-term plan.

Mid-month we're still navigating frost warnings. One night the local orchard shares a post on social media about how the outcome of their entire crop hinges on the wind. It's been relentless, and the sound drones on for hours, and yet if it stops, the frost will attack and the apple crops, as well as so many others like blueberry, strawberry, etc… will be ruined for the year. The damage would be sustained at 27 degrees Fahrenheit. The low drops to 26.6 in the early hours of the morning, and yet, it appears the crops survived.

The peepers are singing loud and clear, even amid the windy nights. I can hear them as I fall asleep, a swampy symphony.

The week after Mother's Day, all the early spring plants are in bloom. There's a huge difference between the colors up near the house, where everything looks brighter, and the colors in the fields where the vastness takes over, and mostly what you see is green. But if you're in the middle of it, you see the brilliance of the dandelions. If you slow down you can see the subtle colors hiding in the ground cover of the woods. There are whites and blues, and down low you can catch views of violets and the white of flowering strawberries. The landscape is overwhelmed by green, but like a Where's Waldo book, there are details that make you smile if you look close enough.

Down on one of the paths that go from Upper Field to Lower Field is the branch that was left behind from one of the storms. Last month I noticed the buds that survived the winter. Now, the stored energy has created blossoms. While the branch is broken, it still blooms.

Two weeks post-concussion, I start to feel more like myself once again though I'm reminded through a phone consultation with my nurse practitioner that while they're subtle, I still have symptoms from the injury, and to take it slowly. She tells me that once I hit my threshold, to stop and try again the next day. The next day? I ask, incredulous. The next day, she reiterates.

That same week Lucas's parents, Mary Lou and Ted, return to Maine from their three-season home in Florida. Lucas picks them up from the Portland airport and brings them to our house for a quick visit and meal before sending them on their way down to the coast to their condo where we'll visit with them over the summer months. We used to spend long weekends, but now with the dog and the rabbits, it's harder to get away as our lifestyle and commitments have changed from our pet free and rental days.

For the last few years, ever since they moved from a house on the side of a mountain in New Hampshire, their arrival has signified the unofficial start of the transition from spring to summer. It coincides with the kids finishing up schoolwork for the year, longing for beach days whether at the coast or lakeside, and warmer temperatures. And with the kids finishing up their school work, the space that's taken up in my brain by those tasks opens. Historically this is when I feel the push to create, to write, more than any other time of the year as there's more space for me to explore my own pursuits. And so the pull to my desk is strong, even though the computer is not the best friend of a concussed writer.

But the blooms, the sunshine, and the reminders of the shift in seasons seem to spur on my energy. There's more laughter, more pep in my step, and more time spent doing. While slow and steady have been my mantra, my soul is ready for something different. My head knows I need to go gently, but my heart wants to move, wants to be back in the dailiness, and wants to stop relying on other people to do the things my injury has held me back from.

For all the times I have complained about the daily chores, the errands that high school-age kids require, the going going going, there's a part of me that desperately misses it. There's a large piece of me that misses what was our norm.

I get swept up in the rhythms of late spring, and ignore my threshold. I go past it, many times. And so it's no surprise that just as the first wave of blooms starts to fade, my recovery takes a nosedive. I wake up feeling dizzy for the first time since the injury occurred, and for the rest of the week, I'm back to needing daily naps.

After a week of feeling down in the dumps, unable to show up at my desk in the way that I want to, I go outside to water the rhododendrons and catch sight of the

131

next wave of growth. There's a handful of buds on the cusp of blossoming and one that is fully open. Its deep magenta hints at summer dresses and fruit punch. Across the driveway, the lilacs are halfway to full, their scent wafts towards me in a cloud of childhood memories of growing up on the seacoast of New Hampshire where lilacs are as common as hydrangeas on Cape Cod in summertime. The heads atop iris stalks creep out of their hoods, and a deep purple flower is on its way to revealing itself.

The spring blooms, much like recovery, come in waves.

Looking back at the month it feels like it dragged on in long mornings and afternoons spent napping, resting, staring at the ceiling, but it equally passed as quickly as the azalea bush's flowers. What I have to show for May is a simple knit shawl that kept my hands busy and my mind peaceful, knit throughout the last few weeks, and these words that have amassed in fits and spurts copied first into handwritten journal entries before being entered onto the computer. I also have a brain that has mostly settled down and nestled into place, and an awareness of how quickly life can change. There is gratitude for the privilege of rest - though mandated - and even more gratitude for family and friends who encourage healing over anything else.

As I dip my toes back into regular work, I find myself coming back to what I thought of in the hours before my injury: honoring and protecting the choices one makes in life, and I'm thinking about what falls away and doesn't need to be picked up again after a break. These weeks spent largely convalescing have shown me just what happens when the chores I so often let get in my way of writing don't happen. Nothing. It's shown me what happens when you don't respond to texts and emails right away. Nothing. It reminded me that reacting to life as it's happening is a much more chaotic way of being than allowing the seasons to unfold, recognizing where you have choices, and how to make them from an empowered place of acceptance and curiosity instead of reactivity.

The last weekend of May we spend an evening around the portable fire pit we've placed in the yard. The kids bring out their instruments, Paige on the guitar, Fynn on bass, and Lucas brings out fixings for s'mores. Darcey wanders around and settles as the fire crackles and the kids play versions of Red Hot Chili Pepper songs. There's laughter, and also interruptions as my parent's washing machine is on the fritz, so my father comes back and forth a few times looking for the wet vac, the very same tool I was using at the beginning of the month. It's all the makings of a life, these very real moments of laughter and bliss and interruptions and togetherness in unexpected yet welcome ways.

As the daylight fades I settle into the chair, hug my sweatshirt closer around myself as a slight chill descends, and look around. The irises that are planted close to the house have started opening, and the hydrangea bushes that were a mess of brown frost-touched leaves are now growing back in shocks of green that play against the golden wood chip mulch. Out front, the rhododendrons we planted a few weeks ago are covered in flowers, with more to come.

Hours later I'm in bed, freshly showered but the smell of campfire still lingers. I close my eyes and fall into the deepest sleep I've had for weeks. I wake up not necessarily with a spring in my step but with a hopeful eye on June and so much gratitude and softness for May.

June

The first of June falls on a Thursday, and the temperatures are predicted to be in the 90s, so the kids and I plan for a trip to the coast once again. This whole week the temperatures have been above average, and we've traded out jeans for shorts and dresses, long sleeves are saved for our walks through the woods to fend off the mosquitoes and black flies. We pack a fruit salad and sandwiches and make the hour-long drive to Wolf's Neck Woods State Park in Freeport.

I'm still feeling shaky about driving, as concentrating on the road takes as much of a toll as watching screens, so Fynn and I decide to split the driving. He's working on accumulating the 70 hours behind the wheel needed to apply for his license. He takes the drive out and tells me he can do the one back if I don't feel up for it. Through May it became ever so clear how much more I can rely on the kids, how they're up for more tasks than I had been willing to give them or admit they were capable of handling.

Of course, he drives cautiously and navigates the various driving conditions smoothly. We go through Auburn where the big box stores and highways live, multiple lanes of traffic, and the downtown areas. From there we head out through farmlands that follow the river that leads to the coast. After Auburn comes Durham, and then Freeport where there's more traffic, more construction, more stores, and tourists to dodge. After we get off the main road we wind down towards the state park where the trees become more sparse, though still there, and the properties are dotted with signs of coastal living - views of marshes, cape-style houses, shake siding, as well as a splattering of lupines and rhododendrons like the ones we planted last month in our yard. The flowers are brilliant against the houses.

When we arrive at the park we grab our bags and take the wooded path that's marked with an arrow pointing to the Casco Bay Trail. We walk over a stream where the area is densely populated with trees, and then the trail opens up to views of the water. I've been here only a few times before, but each time - this one included - I gasp at the view. The park sits on a peninsula that runs between the Harraseeket River and the Casco Bay. The trail we've taken leads us to the type of beach that is synonymous with the Maine coastline, rocky and full of tidal pools with a backdrop of pine trees. We find a shady spot and throw our blanket down on the rounded rocks and weathered shells. The outgoing tide reveals massive formations of rocks, and tide pools where two families with small children are exploring. Across the way is an island, and though it wouldn't be hard to get to when the tide is out, it's clearly marked with signs to keep off, not just for people's safety but because it's a nesting site for osprey.

But the thing that is most striking, aside from the sun and the unseasonable temperatures, is the smell. The combination of seaweed and salt air is comforting and elicits a sigh from all three of us. We need nothing more but to sit and close our eyes, basking in our surroundings.

The families that are exploring the tide pools break our reverie. The children exclaim over horseshoe crabs, the parents point out muscles and hermit crabs, and one of the fathers boldly dives under the frigid water and is met with cheers from the children.

From beside me, Paige says, "They're totally

homeschoolers."

Given that school is still in session in our area,
her observation is an educated guess that I would agree
with. There's also something in the way the parents are
interacting with their kids, a freedom and unhurried-ness
that aligns with some homeschooling philosophies, though
it's not exclusive to families that choose to educate their
children in a certain way. At the end of my eleventh year
of this homeschool gig, and nearly seventeen years of
parenting, I know better than to blankly judge anything
when it comes to education, children, or other parents.
There is always more to the story than what we see, always.

What I do know is the way the parents are
adventuring with their children, following the little one's
leads, encouraging them to leap and jump and get dirty and
be in the wilderness reminds me of when my two were little
and we'd spend hours at the shoreline looking at seashells.
I kept tabs on the worry I felt as they adeptly leaped from
one rock to another, so as not to feel I was holding them
back, and also felt the genuine delight and awe that passed
between us when they found some sort of beach treasure,
whether it was driftwood, moon snails, or an abandoned
sand toy.

Now they're sitting on the beach blanket, staying

out of the sun and the tide pools. Fynn's napping on and off, and Paige is reading a graphic novel. I'm the one who feels the need to move around, to put my feet in the water, to explore. I stand up and ask if either of them wants to walk around, they both decline.

I dip my toes at the water's edge. Because we're in a protected area, the water is warmer than you'd expect from the Atlantic Ocean in June. There's seaweed to step around, barnacle-covered rocks to dodge, and crabs just beneath the sand ready to pinch soft flesh. And yet, all that considered, being here in this moment feels like a slice of heaven.

I make my way to a big rock and take a seat, looking out at the bay. The small children and their parents have gone around a bend, and it's grown quiet. Fynn makes his joins me, and after a moment he tells me he's glad we came. Eventually, Paige puts down her book and starts to explore the rocks, her long limbs carry back and forth to us and the water's edge as she finds treasures by way of small crabs she holds between her pointer finger and thumb to show us. This is the way they are, him with his quiet but comfortable presence, her with an ability to lighten any situation with her laughter and curiosity.

The hour drive home looms and we don't stay much

longer. We pack our things into the car, and I have a fleeting memory of buckling the kids into car seats, kissing their shoulders, and tasting salt water on their sun-kissed skin. I settle for giving them sideways hugs and am thankful for the dark sunglasses to hide the sniffed-back tears that threaten to fall. There's a constant duality in our days, the past lingers while the present is so very full.

The unseasonable weather continues, except it swings the other way. A storm front comes in and brings with it cool temperatures, the lows extending into the forties, the highs in the fifties. With the dampness of continued rain, the cold sinks even more deeply than usual thanks to the warm temperatures we experienced just days earlier. The rain stays with us, and it feels like we're back to those weeks in late April and the beginning of May when it rained so much the fields flooded. But now we're not getting the heavy rains, just drizzles spread out over days with occasional heavier showers. The gray looms, the sunshine hidden, and the bones chill.

It feels like ever since that first day of May, I've been waiting for the rain to stop. What if I stopped waiting for the rain to end, to start living? What if instead of waiting for it to stop, I got back to that person who wanted to take the dog for walks in the rain? What if instead of looking from inside the safe, warm, and dry house, I danced in the rain?

Summer, without the backdrop of the kid's studies, opens up space for my writing and brings with it possibilities. The novel I've been skirting around, prodding at occasionally, beckons fully. Yes, we have commitments, but we also have expanses of time, and the previous sense of urgency blurs at the hour's edges.

I start editing the novel in earnest. I reread it, write a structural outline, and start poking at the plot holes. This month contains a bit of everything, including swaths of empty and unplanned days, but my focus and attention are elsewhere, on upcoming trips and appointments, everything outward, rather than inward. It's almost like having too much time at the ready allows for too many choices, too many rabbit holes to go down, and distractions to take hold. The possibilities are overwhelming, in life but also in my fictional world - especially within a second draft.

The question of how many directions can a story take is not unlike the one that asks how many ways can you spend a summer. For some, the expansion is a gift. For others, a sense of overwhelm lingers in the open spaces.

Outside the rain continues, our walks are stinted, our energy becomes more melancholy as the days go on. The lack of urgency, the fewer to-do's, and the upcoming but not quite yet plans, all combine into a sense of almost paralysis. Where does one start? Where does one go? Is there a point in beginning when it'll all be on hold in a few days?

Early in the month, my parents pack up their car and head south to Pennsylvania to visit my mother's family. The day they leave we hear reports that the air quality will be impacted by smoke from the Canadian wildfires. We watch the skies, but they're only overcast. I overhear Lucas answering questions on a work call, "No, so far we're north of it all." Midday I start to get texts with photos from my mother. From Connecticut onward the drive was muddled with orange skies and decreased visibility. News from New York City comes through, and photos of people

wearing masks not for the still ongoing pandemic, but
for air quality, flood our news feeds. The city draped in
an orange filter looks otherworldly, but while even in the
southern part of Maine they are seeing effects, here in the
central part of the state the currents protect the air and the
only thing inhibiting our time outdoors is the onslaught of
mosquitoes and black flies.

While they're away, I'm charged with tending to
my parent's gardens. There's a vegetable garden, a small
patch of rhubarb behind the barn, peas on the side of the
house starting to twist up a tripod, hanging baskets to
water, and plants still in their packaging from the garden
center, waiting to be planted later in the month. Inside there
are plants on a shelf decked out with grow lamps: cosmos,
tomatoes, peppers, and marigolds, still making their way
into the world in the gentlest way possible. A handwritten
list of to-do's in Mom's script sits on their kitchen counter.
We went over it before they left, and I watched as my
mother did her daily dance between the sink and the shelf,
watering each tray in a methodical and tried and true
manner.

Thanks to the rain, I haven't had to water the plants
too often. But the moment I step foot into my Mom's
world, I can feel her with me, across all those miles,

encouraging me to stick my finger in the dirt - a good two inches - to see what needs watering. With dirt under my nails, mosquitoes and black flies at my arms, rain boots covered with grass clippings, and fighting with the coil of hose behind me, I can't help but smile and look around in awe. The growing season where we are in Maine is slower to start and shorter in length than even an hour south, and while the garden is still in its early days of the year, it's filled with so much potential and hard work, so much planning and hope.

Standing in the middle of the vegetable garden, potatoes on one side of me, lettuce, carrots, and beets on the other, it amazes me that all of this started with a dream and packages of seeds. It's not unfamiliar with the way I've often thought about the making of our lives, and how we choose to live each day. It starts with dreams and choices sometimes so minute we might miss them if we weren't paying close enough attention. Choosing to take a breath instead of rushing. Choosing what elements of a meal to make from scratch or which to buy prepared. Choosing what time we wake up, and when it's time to rest. Choosing the people we surround ourselves with, and what relationships to let go. A million choices, and they all start with a dream, an image in our heads, a glimmer of hope.

After watering, I grab Darcey and we take our morning walk. Just as we pass the vegetable garden we both stop in our tracks at the sound of a woodpecker, just up ahead. The trees are thick, and I can't spot the bird, but it's busy at work and doesn't stop even as we start to move toward the tree line. Down the path and into the fields there's more birdsong, alerting others of our coming. I can make out chickadees, but the rest blend. Earlier in the year I was overwhelmed by the names of all the plants, but slowly I can feel a library of terms and names building in my mind. I hope the same happens for bird songs and calls, though my timeline for learning is extending far beyond me, unlike the knowledge I'm trying to impart to my children before they leave the nest. My mind is flooded with choices, what seem like necessities, but when I'm surrounded by gentle breezes and birdsong it all seems so much simpler. Maybe the biggest thing I can impart to my growing children is awareness. Maybe the most important gift I can give is the knowledge that seasons and time unfold with or without our approval or participation, but with awareness we have an opportunity to live in this world with another layer of appreciation. The embodiment we bring to our experience is what allows for a different way of life, a depth that creates space for our timing mixed with that around us, and space for our own experience paired with the natural world that lives within us as much as outside of us if we just get out of our man-made way.

When Darcey and I return from our walk, I let her inside and then walk around the outside of our house. There's a small garden on the corner of our yard and the driveway that includes an ornamental fruit tree, a boulder, and a variety of plants. Last year we found planters made of half barrels near the woods and went to bring them over to this garden for some added visual interest and to use as planters, only to find they were rotted and decaying. Out of the three, one was in good enough condition to be moved, and now it sits in this small garden filled with strawberry plants. Our first spring here we were anxious to see what spring flowers would come up, as I've mentioned before - we'd only seen the property from a dry late June onward. We knew there were daylilies, hostas, and sedum. We were pretty sure there were irises.

As spring came in full, irises were indeed sprinkled around the house and in every side garden. The surprise came not in the amount, but in a small patch of white irises, only a half dozen or so, in an otherwise purple display. While not uncommon in the gardening world, they feel like a happy accident in this setting, and my curiosity is piqued

146

regarding their provenance. Maybe a stray bulb or two made its way into the pack, or maybe the previous owner wanted a bit of something different. Maybe I'll ask the next time I run into them at the grocery store. They moved a few miles up the road, and have been happy to tell us the history of the house, many times over.

Or perhaps I'll let my imagination run wild. Some things are better left unknown. I've found those are the ones that become a part of our story more readily. They aren't flanked by memories of past owners, or past lives. At one point it felt like everyone we met in town had something to do with our house, had stories about it, or had lived in it. Some of the stories left me unsettled, and I had to remind myself that what matters is what's happening here now, what life we bring to the house, and what we do with it moving forward.

With a quick Google search, I learn that purple irises symbolize wisdom and royalty, and white irises purity and innocence. Maybe, amid all the stories and knowledge that's been passed to us, there's a need for a palette cleanser, a blank slate, a childlike curiosity that cuts through what has been to remind us of possibility inspired by wonder.

Upon their return nearly a week later, I stand

outside flanked by my parents as they survey the landscape. I'm surprised at their surprise, as the changes I've seen are tiny in comparison to the words they're exclaiming. To their eyes, things have grown in leaps and bounds. To mine, they've been consistent. I can see where the lettuce has started growing from the cuts Paige made when gathering for the bunnies a few days ago, but otherwise, it all looks like, between my time spent watering and the rain, I've maintained the status quo. Nonetheless, I take the praise they dish out over how well the gardens look, as if it's all because of my handiwork, though I know their gratitude goes beyond the surface of tending to the vegetables and flowers.

The weekend before my parents come home and a few days before I leave on a trip of my own, we try to spend time as a family of four. With two teenagers and two adults, sometimes our attempts at togetherness fall flat, and others find us crying with laughter over the tiniest thing. Earlier Lucas picked up marshmallows, chocolate, and graham crackers from the store, he's determined to have a fire and s'mores. While the Solo stove gets going the kids set up a game of cornhole in the driveway. During the pandemic, we bought a travel set, made of PVC pipes and a fabric base that wraps around the pipes and secures with velcro.

Later in the week, I'm heading to Asheville. I'll be joining two writer friends who have become soul sisters to me for a few days of writing, sightseeing, and simply being together. I've been writing online with these women for over a year, and have known one for nearly a decade, but have yet to meet them in person. Because of the lingering effects of last month's concussion, I choose not to drive as I originally planned. Instead, I'll be taking a bus to the airport, then flying from Logan to Washington, DC, from DC to Pittsburgh, and then driving with friends down to North Carolina. I haven't traveled in such a way, or to such lengths, since before the pandemic. My stomach, which is unwieldy on its best days, is starting to feel the effects of the impending stress even before I get out my suitcase.

I sit in my puddle of stress while the kids toss bags at one another. Darcey watches, her head going back and forth with each of the kid's tosses. Lucas pokes at the fire. My arms are crossed in front of me, and I rock back and forth in the rocking chair, noticing where its white paint is chipping on the sides of the handles.

The kids finish their game, and next up it's me against Fynn. I'm slow to warm up, always have been, and while sometimes I can get in a groove, this evening I can't. But a few turns in I at least feel my body loosening up, my smile growing easier. While my throws are all over the place, Fynn's are consistent and he's got the accumulated points to show for it. There's hardly ever a time when movement doesn't allow for an energy shift, and tonight is no exception. There's an ease in my shoulders when I sit down after Fynn wallops me in cornhole.

Later we're too tired to shower off the scent of campfire and bug spray. It lingers through the night when we wake to howls of coyotes in the distance, and well into the next morning.

Slowly, I pack my bags for the trip. I find myself cursing the decision to not drive myself, frustrated with the lack of books and journals and knitting projects I can take. There are piles of books I want to share with my friends, but instead, I limit myself to my Kindle for reading, a small bag with a simple shawl in progress, and indulge myself with three journals. And then, when I start to pack my clothes, I falter. There's nothing like packing for a trip that sends my sense of style and self into a tizzy, and I think back to the photo album I have on my phone that's filled with outfits I feel myself in. After several deep breaths, and reminders that the women I'll be with know me almost as well as I know myself, that they don't care what I wear, just that I'm there, fully as myself, I get started. I pack the things I feel most myself in: my hand knits, a pair of jeans, a pair of pants that could be mistaken for a skirt, and a sun dress.

On the day of my departure, Lucas takes me to the bus stop, only to find the schedule has changed, and the ticket I printed out just last night no longer has a bus attached to it. There's a mad dash to find another way to the airport, a group effort from those on the homestead to get me where I'm going. My send-off now includes Paige and my mother, a drive to New Hampshire, then a bus to Massachusetts. Somehow it all feels fitting, and I keep my composure and look at it as getting the travel glitches out early in the day instead of looking at the mishap as a foreboding sense of the day ahead. It's a reminder that I'm not in anything alone, even my solo travel days. In that, I find comfort.

I had forgotten what it was like to navigate airports, the smell of an airplane full of late-day travel bodies, and the exhilarating feel of take-off. I marvel at the world from up above the castle like clouds and watch in awe as parents quell tantrums and soothe babes to sleep.

Allison meets me at the airport, and the strangeness of meeting someone in the flesh for the first time quickly fades away with teary eyes and warm embraces. As we drive to her house for the night before meeting our other friend, Gina, we reach out and touch one another and keep saying "You're real!" The following day, we meet Gina at a rest area off the highway, and as the three of us embrace, it feels like coming home.

While with my friends I am reminded of the power of connection, what it's like to be able to reach out and touch the person you're talking with, and what it feels like to sit in a cabin among friends who truly get you, without having to worry about throwing on a bra or feeling like you have to be someone you're not. In Asheville there is a stark contrast to my daily life in Maine, the city life is vibrant and abundant, a feast for the senses. We eat out and walk the streets, meander through bookshops and in and out of boutiques, and two of us even stop for new tattoos by the woman who was the first female tattoo artist in Asheville over thirty years ago. Our tattoos are different from each other, but each includes lavender flowers. For the rest of the trip we find lavender everywhere, a sprig of it laying in the middle of a city sidewalk, lavender lemonade on menus, everywhere we turn our friendships are affirmed.

While our cabin sits just a fifteen-minute drive from downtown, it's surrounded by woods and gardens, with the mountains peaking through the trees. There are cool mornings spent on the porch with hot mugs of tea in hand and slow waking moments turn into hours spent in conversation. There's laughter and tears, and the unwavering sense that we are all seen and heard and understood deeply.

And then in a whirlwind and far too soon, I am home again. While we were blessed with mostly sunshine in North Carolina, the weather in Maine has been filled with rain showers which did nothing but help the growth of all the things. The wildflower meadow is a foot taller than when I left, my hydrangeas and my parent's hibiscus - both of which we weren't sure were going to make it after the heavy snow and late frost - have taken off and are full of summer's potential, and the vegetable garden is coming to life in all directions and ways.

I arrive home on a Tuesday and to an empty calendar for the week, thinking in advance that I would need time to rest from travel, to adjust. The first morning back happens to be the first day of summer, and after wandering the house a bit feeling like I've lost a limb, looking for early conversation and my cabin mates, I take Darcey for a long walk, stopping to talk with my parents at the garden. They have projects they want to show me, the garden to show off. Mom tells me I look refreshed, that I must have needed the trip. There's a bounce in my step that matches Darcey's, and I'm questioning the idea behind the empty calendar, as I'm feeling ready to go with all the things. After talking about creativity and writing for days, I want to hang on to the positivity, and the support that one gets from being surrounded by other writers and artists. There's the feeling of being in a bubble of positivity and support, and not wanting to burst it. I side-step land mines of conversation in the day-to-day, at home and the grocery store, wanting to preserve the inspiration and forward momentum.

I hang onto it and the first whispers of summer, though they're hidden in gray skies and the threatening rain, for the first few days. But towards the end of the week while I'm working, writing in the office I share with my husband, as well as online with the same friends who I was sitting with just days ago in the flesh, the bubble bursts and I feel an overwhelming pang of heaviness and loss and frustration in my chest. It comes when I'm trying to have a conversation with my friends who I look at as co-workers in some respects, having an in-depth conversation that requires attention, but I have to move from my desk, my space, because of one of Lucas's work calls. I move to another room, only to have to move once more when Paige comes downstairs and starts her morning routine of washing lettuce in the kitchen for the bunnies, and then using the lettuce spinner. It's too much noise and so I move again, this time into the bedroom. I can still hear Lucas's voice, the lettuce spinner, and once more I get up from my spot and close a door that doesn't fully latch, knowing the dog will make her way in shortly, frustration etched on my face.

One of the many conversations we had in Asheville was about needing space to create, literally and figuratively.

155

We all spoke about our own creative spaces, and what we thought we might be able to do to create a more welcoming space for our words, our work. When it came to my space, I mentioned that I wanted to move my desk to a spot where I could simply be, regardless of what I was doing or working on. We brainstormed about different spaces in the house, even use of the cabin more regularly. But by the time I got home, I was no closer to figuring out where I could create a slice of quiet.

The cabin, while it's a quiet, secluded space, is not my own. It's a shared entity that is for all, and it has absorbed the energy of family, of togetherness, of play. It's fine for a visit, even short bouts of work, but the way it is now, with hard chairs and no toilet facilities, it does not lend itself to a consistent writing space. I've used it for a make-shift at-home writing retreat and felt like I spent more time walking back and forth to the house for the bathroom than actually getting into the groove of writing.

Then there's the question of does one really need a perfect space? Is it unattainable and a form of procrastination? But when it comes down to it, I know that there's a true need because of how my body reacts when there's a disruption. In my body, it feels like a betrayal, like I'm abandoning my needs for everyone else's, and my needs as a writer are needs that are entirely entrenched in my needs as a person. And when we have unmet needs, they grow from a whisper until they become a full-on shout, turning into a disruption far more potent than that of a salad spinner.

Today, quiet lands in a corner of our bedroom where currently, there's a cabinet full of my hand knits, but I look around the room, the closet space, the floor space, to see where things can be moved. I start by making room in our closet for a dresser and then proceed to slide one dresser across our fake wood linoleum floors into it. Next, the hand knit sweater cabinet slides into the place of the old dresser, and the corner I have my eye on is empty except for dust bunnies mixed with dog hair.

In a spurt of energy, I start moving my half of the office. Piles of books, a bunch of shelves on wheels, my laptop, a stationary monitor, and the talismans on my desk, all make their way from one room into the other. The desk comes next, and it fits perfectly in the corner, and when I take my seat I have a window to the left in front of me, and one to the right behind me. Finally, the pictures and bulletin board are hung, and a strand of twinkle lights is plugged in. There's softness and spaciousness in this corner.

I snap a few pictures and send them to my creative

cohorts. Their responses come quickly and are full of encouragement. Their energy infuses into the corner in a supported way that is inexplicable and yet true.

While not entirely a room of my own, it's a quiet corner in a room that's barely used throughout the day. I'll take it, and I can't wait to see what it feels like to be on my schedule, permitting me to work whenever, and however, feels right. And after sitting in the space for even just a few moments, a candle and the small lights glowing, it feels more right than I could have imagined.

On a Sunday afternoon, before the rain and thunderstorms, I sneak outside to the hayfield behind our house and cut flowers for the kitchen windowsill, some tufted vetch and maiden pink.

Out front the rhododendrons catch my eye, the flowers have turned brown and have started to fall to the ground. From afar it looks like weeds are growing out from the center of the plant, and I walk over to investigate. To my surprise, the gangling shoots are new growth, its leaves are the telltale nearly oval shape of the others, and the texture is the same as the established leaves. It's just that the color hasn't quite caught up to the rest of the plant, it's a new, lighter, spring green as opposed to the deep green we recognize. The new growth will simply take time to acclimate, blend in, to become a seamless part of the whole.

With flowers in hand, I look down and say to myself, you are *here*. You're here. Living the way you want. Being the way you want. And then there's a moment of pure bliss in the recognition. My skirt swishes around me in the hazy sunshine, and the moment sticks with me like the humidity on my skin.

The travels of the month mixed with the rain, the movement of a few pieces of furniture, and time away from creative projects have made me aware of the splendors and joys of the world, but also the gifts of home. Sometimes when you're so deeply involved in your day-to-day life, it's hard to see what is actually in front of you. Take a few steps back, and the hard work we all put into our lives, the creativity we throw into making a life, new growth as well as the established, it all expands and becomes something truly incredible.

July

The first of July rolls in on a gloomy Saturday. There's no rain, but the sky is gray and overcast. Sunday brings with it rain, all day long, heavy in spots. Someone mentions that it's an El Niño year, and finally, the rain of the last few months makes sense. We're just days into summer, and already we're talking about what an El Niño year means for the upcoming winter. This June ended up as one of the rainiest ones on record for Maine, it's hard not to start wondering what the winter months have in store.

We quip about the fact that our first year with solar panels is bringing an onslaught of rain. The dampness never seems to go away, and each morning I wonder if we'll roll over and find moss growing on our shoulders.

After seemingly months of showers, poor Darcey has had enough. It's the third of July, and knowing there

160

will be fireworks down the road tonight, we're desperate for her to expend her excess anxiety and energy. When there seems to be a break in the rain, Lucas and I take her out for a walk, only to be halfway into it to feel water droplets on our arms. We look at each other and shrug, Darcey is running up ahead, and our clothes will dry. We walk on.

We both wear glasses, and by the time we're home we can barely see, wishing for tiny windshield wipers that could attach to our lenses. Inside Darcey follows us closely, starting to tremble even though she was just outside in the rain with no problem. What seems to bother her is how the rain falls on the roof, the sound it makes. We hoped that the solar panels might change the sound, lift some of her worries, but that hasn't been the case.

Later that same day, after both Darcey and I had dried off and enjoyed a brief couch nap, the weather clears. And by clears, I mean it's not raining. There are still clouds, it's still overcast. The last few weeks have felt like we were back in the pandemic, where we were home for days on end. Yes, we have the freedom to go out now, but the weather, the dog, it all seems like too much. Fynn and I have a brief conversation about how we miss having the beach to go to in every type of weather or our favorite parks back in Massachusetts.

"I miss knowing where to go out," I tell him. He nods in understanding. "Do you want to try a new walk today? There's a trail not far away."

He shrugs his shoulders and says, "Sure," but I think it's a hard sell. When we reconvene for our walk, I offer just a trek to the fields, he says yes right away.

It's been a while since the two of us went for a walk together and included Darcey, but in the past few months her off-leash walking has been less energetic and more relaxed, and she listens well. For a while when I'd go for walks with the kids I'd leave Darcey behind, as I wanted to be sure to catch any and all moments of conversations with the kids. I wanted to be present. Now, she saunters along with us as though she's part of the conversation, and in many ways she is.

On the way down to the fields from Hobbit Hill there's a break in the clouds, and we all stop - at least two of us for the same reason - and laugh at the fact that it's been so long since we've seen blue sky. I tell Fynn I want to see the fields, maybe the Bucket Trail. With the rainy weather, we've stuck to our walk down Chickadee Lane and up Sledding Hill toward home. While we won't leave the property, there's ways to satisfy my craving for adventure right here.

We go around the close side of Lower Field and head down the Bucket Trail. It looks like the path had flooded not that long ago, the ground is squishy beneath our feet, and there's more sand strewn across the pine needles than there had been the last time I was here. Darcey cautiously walks a little bit ahead but waits for us when I stop to take pictures. At one point Fynn walks close to the river on a narrow sand bank, but I stay up on the trail. Darcey goes to the edge of the trail and keeps an eye on Fynn, making sure he's safe. She looks back at me as if to say, "He's still good!" and when he gets a little too close to the water she looks at me with her ears perked up. "He's fine," I tell her, just as much as I have to tell myself most days.

Eventually, the mosquitoes find us. They're worse than they were the last two summers, of course, because of all the rain. They've had nothing but time to breed and thrive and sit patiently waiting for innocent victims to cross their paths. Out of the wooded trail and into the open field we go. The hay is nearly as tall as I am, higher than I think I've ever seen it. The floods from May did nothing to hinder its growth like we suspected they might. The hay gets cut generally around the fourth of July, and then again around Labor Day each year. The caveat to that is that there needs to be three days of dry conditions to do the work, and even the weather forecasters are talking about how much the hay farmers need dry weather - a flip from the previous few years of drought.

The hay is so tall that we can't find the path that my father normally clears from one side of the field to the other. We keep waiting to stumble across it, Darcey looks back at us time and time again like we've walked past it, but it isn't there.

"She's cut through!" cries Fynn, and so I call the dog back, not sure if she'll come or not. There's a brief feeling of panic over her in the middle of the hayfield, the thousands of ticks she'll end up with, if we can ever get her out of the hay. But then she comes prancing back to us, tongue hanging out of a big grin. She found the path. Even a few yards ahead of us, we couldn't see it. But she could.

The blue sky has gone behind the clouds once again, and the humidity has risen as much as the temperatures. By the time we make it home, my skin is sticky with sweat and bug spray, but at least our glasses aren't covered in water droplets.

We have two days of sunshine and 80-plus-degree weather in a row. A wall of humidity hangs heavy. With the extremes of the weather and temperature fluctuation, we don't know if we're coming or going, if this is summer or just a fluke.

The kids are taking their end-of-the-year evaluations. It's later than usual, but as they're not due until August we decide to take our time. Previously scheduled, it feels fitting that they end up on the two days of the week when we're due for beautiful summer-like weather before going back into a deluge of swampy humidity. They finish by lunchtime, so our afternoons are free. On the first day, even though it feels like we should take advantage of the sun, we have errands to do. The grocery store calls, the post office beckons, and then by the time we get home I can see it written all over Paige's face that she needs a break. There will be no outdoor adventure this afternoon.

The next day the kids work through their second and final day of testing. In the afternoon I offer a trip to the lake, but there are no takers. One kid's stomach doesn't feel well, and the other has used all their brain power and just wants to recharge in their room. I consider my options: stay or go by myself. I waver for a moment, feeling the ever-present pull of home and the path of least resistance, but then decide to heed the call of the water and pack a bag for myself. In it go the bare necessities: a towel, a book, knitting, suntan lotion, and a bottle of water.

It's a twenty-minute drive down twisty back roads, and the public beach of Lake Anasagunticook, otherwise known as Canton Lake, is right off the main road and so narrow and brief that you might miss it if you blinked. It's nearly three in the afternoon and there's a smattering of families and couples on the beach and in the water. It's still the week of July 4th, and while I'm not one for crowds, it's heartening to see families on vacation out enjoying the sun.

The beach consists of about two feet of sand, and then there's a wall of rocks that you can climb to the metal barrier between the beach and the road. There are two or three openings for stairs, but there's no lifeguard. There are a few makeshift benches that sit low to the ground. It's rustic but charming.

I make my way around a few piles of beach towels and find an open bench. There's a couple to my left, a trio of little girls with their grandfather to my right. The girls are playing around a motorboat that's been brought up to shore that the grandfather is tinkering with.

First things first, I slip out of my clothes and into the water. Even though we've had rain and temperatures have fluxed, the last two days of pure sunshine have turned the lake into bath water. It doesn't seem like it could be refreshing, but then I dive in and float on my back for a while, feeling the breeze and sunshine on my face. It feels as though I've been released from the clenches of the heat.

For the next hour and a half, I alternate between reading, swimming, and knitting. The little girls next to me say hello every once and a while between games of pretend. They draw my attention away from my book with their sweet voices as they ask their grandfather to play. He obliges and sits in the water where the girls flock to him instantly, climbing over him while insisting he partake in their game. His words are quiet, but you can hear the smile in them even from a distance. Eventually, the sun starts getting lower in the sky, and he asks them if they'd like to go back to the house for a snack.

"I have cherries," he says, and the girls cheer. They start to put their life vests on, at the direction of no one, gather their swim goggles and a few rocks, and as they climb in the boat one of them asks, "Why didn't we bring the cherries with us?" The grandfather shrugs and says, "I didn't think about it." His answer is accepted easily, and off they go, into the boat. The motor starts and in no time they're turning the boat around and waving to everyone on the beach, their smiles so big it looks like they won the lottery. With one hand on the helm, the grandfather uses his free hand to tip his hat to all on shore; they start to drive off across the lake toward home.

After watching the scene unfold, there are tears brimming in my eyes, thinking about the ease between the four of them, marveling at the memories those girls will have of their grandfather, wondering about the circumstances that created the levels of comfort and trust between them.

I turn back to my book, Maia Toll's *Letting Magic In*, and read the final few pages. At one point I look in my bag for a pencil or pen, but come up empty-handed. So instead, I reread a passage several times, committing it to memory so I'll remember to underline it when I get home.

"After a lifetime of looking, I'd finally stepped into my own story. I'd found the magic I'd been looking for."

Isn't that what we're all after, a bit of magic in our lives? And that phrase, "I'd stepped into my own story," stays with me when I take a final dip, and as I surface and look around at the mountains surrounding the lake. It stays with me as I drip dry while knitting a few stitches on the shawl, noticing the contrast and saturation of the different hues of purple in the yarn against the deep blue of the sky, the green of the trees, and the depths of the water. It stays with me as I turn the radio up on the way home, and lose my voice from singing as loud as I can down roads that have become familiar. It stays with me even when I come home, kids still holed up in their rooms, Lucas still at his work desk, and I jump into the shower to wash sunscreen and sand off my skin, leaving behind the softness that comes from a few hours spent in the fresh air and lake water. And it stays with me as I get to work on dinner, as my hair drips down onto my shoulders, and I move into another part of my day, another part of my story.

Over the weekend, the humidity is at 93 percent. The air is so thick that when the dog farts the smell stays right above her like a little rain cloud. Mom sends a picture of a morning glory over in the vegetable garden. I promise to go see it, but by the time I get there, it's curled back in on itself.

The stillness of summer mirrors the stillness of

winter. The same disconnect of January with resolutions and hibernation can be felt in the busyness and yet slowness the heat of July brings and demands. The summer months are so similar to winter in the extremes. Feeling shut up in the house because of humidity and heat is akin - to me - to the weekend we spent inside during the winter when the temperature dipped well below zero and frost clung to the inside walls.

It's the start of a weeklong staycation for Lucas, one of a few he's taking this summer, and so we try to pepper activities during the week to take advantage of all that's around us, a reminder that we don't have to travel far to enjoy the state we live in, while staying close enough to tend to our animals. When we first moved to Maine I had no idea about all the towns that were named after international locations. There's Paris, Mexico, Poland, China, Belfast, Peru, and more. This morning we're starting off in Norway, with the Norway Music and Art Festival. Mom comes with us for our adventure and both kids set their alarms to join as well. We arrive early to beat the heat, but it and the humidity catch up to us. Regardless, we spend longer than any of us thought we would visiting vendors. There's photographers and ceramic artists, woodworkers and painters, tents run by the county Democrats, and

others by the local theater company. There's something for
everyone, and we walk separately and then together, finding
each other in the crowd. We fill our arms with purchases
and our minds with stories from local crafters. These are
the things that help us to feel connected, to make small talk
with people who live nearby, connecting over what brings
them - and us - joy. Art, community, and ice cold beverages
make a sweltering Saturday all the more enjoyable.

Lucas, Darcey, and I are walking down by the river.
There's a rustle in the trees that startles us. We look to the
left to see a Bald Eagle swoop down from its perch and
soar through the tunnel of trees down the river, its wingspan
seemingly expanding to the width of the Nezinscot.

There's more rain. Vermont, the whole of it, floods
after a day of nine inches of rain and is under a state of
emergency. When the sun finally makes an appearance we
find the hay is matted down with rain, dew hangs to the
strands and when the sun shines on them it looks like there

are fields of sparkling crystals surrounding us.

Lucas and I take a daytrip up to The Lost Kitchen Farmer's Market, just the two of us. Since we both work from home, we're together a lot, but there's something special about heading out in the car together. Even the simplest outing to the grocery store feels like a date, but this time we've set aside during a week of family time, feels extra special. We've spent the past few winters watching The Lost Kitchen, and at home Erin French's name is thrown around like she's a friend of ours. One Christmas the majority of our gifts were Lost Kitchen inspired, from her book *Finding Freedom* to a tea kettle and spice mixture from her online store, her wares were spread under our Christmas Tree. We called it a Lost Kitchen Christmas.

When we arrive I smile as I take it all in. The details are everything. Tiny bud vases on picnic tables, the bicycle with a basket overflowing with flowers, the way the hibiscus rose tea tasted on my tongue. We pick up some goats cheese and locally grown potatoes from the market, a citrus juicer and some notepads from the gift shop, and call it a day as the crowds and heat are a bit much. We've soaked in everything from the waterfall and mill to Erin's smile as she interacts with customers. Our goods and iced beverages in hand, we head back to the car and take a scenic drive home. It's quiet, but we're both content.

Another day during the staycation week we visit Big Falls Preserve. There's mud, so much mud, and more humidity. I'm feeling like I'm moving through water, and am unable to keep up with Lucas and the kids on the hike to the falls. My body is not made for summer, and I'm usually plagued by headaches and other strange body aches and pains, but I wonder if my seasonal headaches are made worse from the lingering effects of my concussion.

We reach the falls, and along with the treetop cover, the water cools us as it rushes by. It's a beautiful backdrop to a fantastic meltdown. I can't help myself, and when we all come together at the falls I start venting a long string of things I'm exhausted by, how I couldn't keep up with them all on the way here and how no one looked back to make sure I was there, how I'm tired of letting go of things. The kids slink away to explore and escape my heat and fatigue induced tirade, but Lucas latches on and suggests that I never let go of anything. If there's something I've let go of, he's not sure what it is. I think of all the things I let go of on a daily basis, and realize we're speaking different languages. He's thinking of the things I point out, the times I ask people to do things a different way in the house, my frustration over dishes not being fully clean or towels folded haphazardly. I'm thinking of eye rolls, interruptions big and small, slights of mouth and actions not intended for me but still felt deeply, things I can't control, one phase of parenting for the next, the way I used to mother small children… and the list goes on. What it comes down to, what it always comes down to, is communication, bridging the gap between the languages we're speaking, and the worlds we inhabit.

There's an undoing by the waterfall, and my tears continue well into and past our drive home. Our marriage is not perfect, but it's built on hearing each other, on not running when things get hard. We give each other space, but then come back to one another, always. The knitting back together will take more than a few hour's time, but with intention and care, we get there. Stitch by stitch. Word by word.

Mid-month, my mother catches us on our way home

from a morning walk. They're pulling the garlic today, she says. She wants to start at eleven. Lucas and the kids are off to the coast to spend time with Mary Lou and Ted, but I'll be home, so I tell her I'll be over. In my mind I'm rearranging my plans, because a day home alone is rare, and the week has gotten away from me because of Lucas's vacation. The house needs cleaning, but more so, I could use a couple of hours in a quiet house to write. I've stuck with my mornings and while everyone knows I write first thing, that doesn't mean I don't write during other parts of the day as well. Those parts, however, are not as protected, and are seen as - and in reality are - more flexible, whereas so many things that need to get done are not. Appointments are set in stone whereas harvesting things in the garden is dependent on weather conditions and the timing of the vegetables, groceries run out… so many needs and to-dos. It's why I protect my morning writing time, but during some seasons, I need more than just an hour or two first thing in the morning.

But today, the garlic needs to be pulled before yet another thunderstorm, so at eleven I head outside to help. My help is not required, but I want to be there. That's the thing, so many of the events that come up that I could say no to are things I want to do. I want to be a part of the garden, I want to be a part of the things that happen on the property, the projects my parents come up with and spearhead. It's just that sometimes they aren't my priority, whereas they are a priority for my parents, and so their timing isn't flexible, just like my morning writing time isn't flexible or up for grabs.

Still feeling the vulnerability from the day before at the falls and the effects of the heat and humidity, I know I'm not bringing high energy to the mix, but I'm present. The three of us head over to the garlic bed and as we approach, the Japanese Beetles swarm. They dive bomb our heads, and while standing still listening to Mom's instructions, one flies down the back of my neck and into my shirt. Mom tells me to hold still, and she fishes it out.

Dad digs into the bed with a pitchfork to loosen the garlic bulbs from the soil. The distinct smell of pickles wafts through the thick, sticky air. There's dill that's grown between the garlic plants, and the combination of scents makes me think of my favorite crisp dill spears.

Mom planted two varieties of garlic this year: Music and German Extra Hardy. But the placards have faded, and it's an educated guess on her part as to which side of the bed is which. We grasp each stalk and pull, the roots hold onto soil as if for dear life. We've spread old sheets on the grass, and place each type of garlic on a separate sheet, with a third for those in the middle which we're unsure of the variety, not knowing where she planted one and started the other.

Mom gasps with excitement over the size of the bulbs when we start - her excitement carries us through harvesting.

We carry the sheets filled with garlic into the barn, where Dad has built a drying rack and placed it on top of a shelf so tall we need a lift to get up there. The basket Dad bought earlier in the year that attaches to the tractor comes into play. It's essentially a cherry picker, the type of equipment used by the electric company to hoist a worker up into the air and reach the wires attached to poles. The one that attaches to the tractor is called a "man basket" and is a metal box painted orange to match the trademark Kubota tractor color. Mom steps into the basket, and from inside the tractor Dad hoists the box, my mother, and the harvest into the air, garlic wafting behind them.

Of all the things I never thought I'd see, this is high up on the list. And yet, as I shake my head and smile, it's not unexpected. I'm reminded of all the times I've watched my parents attempt home improvement and garden projects over the years. The way my father's eyes glimmer with possibility as my mother's mouth turns up in one corner and an eyebrow raises to tell the world "challenge accepted." And it seems like it's always been like this, my father on the ground, making sure it's safe and he's steady, my mother reaching towards a dream, with the safety of their partnership beneath her.

What is showcased in the garlic heady barn is trust, the kind of trust that is made up of years of projects, tears at the proverbial waterfall, the ups and downs of growth, and the continuous stumbling and stitching back together of a marriage.

The next week we're back to our regularly scheduled days, and Lucas is at his desk first thing in the mornings. We're back to our daily walks with Darcey that happen around work calls, and family dinners where we debrief.

On Wednesday the kids and I climb into the car at an early hour, and head south for our seasonal tristate pilgrimage. It's a hazy summer day, and the weather is consistent throughout all three states. The temperature doesn't vary from the coast to inland, something which seems to only happen during these peak summer months, and rarely at that. The orthodontist is our first stop, and then we swing by a park just down from our old house to meet my friend Mindy. Thanks to the wonders of modern technology, we've stayed in touch since I moved, and I dare say we've been in better contact than when we lived ten minutes from one another. Now, we sit on a picnic bench while my kids wander as teenagers do, our conversation is limited to a quick visit and so we volley conversation back and forth in speed rounds of topics, fitting the stories of the summer into bullet points to be revisited at a later date.

This park was the one the kids and I would walk to on days we needed to get out of the house, but didn't want to get into the car. It sits on the Merrimac River, the same that we watched from our bedroom windows, and listened to boats speed down while sitting on the porch with cold drinks and snacks during the summer months when the afternoon sun went past our side of the house. At the park, we'd watch ducks and count boats and throw pinecones into the water, and then we'd walk home again down broken sidewalks and past houses where we never met the neighbors, but we'd grown intimate with how they changed the wreaths on their doors for holidays.

Too quickly, we say goodbye to Mindy, and we

go through the next few errands. Back to the orthodontist to pick up a retainer that had to be made, a quick stop at the general store in town for pickles. At the store we find they've changed the layout completely, there are no longer canned goods for sale, and none of their soup mixes or kitchen decor line the shelves. One room is completely blocked off, and all that's for sale is penny candy, though their ice cream counter is still open.

Down the road there's a new bus stop shelter, it's painted bright orange and yellow.

Subtle changes. This is the first visit, nearly two years out, where we've seen changes that locals would have adjusted to, but for us they're glaringly obvious and almost jarring.

Beach days have been few and far between, so when they come everyone takes advantage of them. We arrive in the early afternoon, too soon to see open parking spaces. We drive up to Wallis Sands, a location I've been to a handful of times, but my kids haven't visited. It's popular for smaller kids as the beach is short and there are plenty of lifeguards. Today it fits the bill as the parking is cheap and ample. The water is cold, due to the last storm that churned up the deep waters; so cold my feet hurt for the first few minutes of wading. Paige by my side, we jump waves and go out up to our thighs. I hold my breath and fall back, the shock of the water is an instant mood changer. When I come up there's salt on my lips, I can feel it on my skin and know the texture of my hair will hold onto the ocean for the remainder of the day. It's cold, but it's a welcome cold. Catching my breath I brace myself for the next waves, though they seem less fierce after immersing fully.

I want to hold onto it all. To recognize the staleness of home when the windows are closed and the AC is on. The headaches that for me are synonymous with summer. The way we can have both, hold both ocean and forest in our palms, in our lives. The way I go to bed that night with salty hair… not wanting to wash off the sea, not yet.

Finally, we get some dry weather. We open the windows, and the house feels expansive again. On Friday I take Darcey out for our morning walk, and I can hear the hum of a tractor down in the fields. We stick to our normal path around Chickadee Lane and up Sledding Hill, but I can look down into Lower Field and see the farmer has cut down half a field's worth of hay. While there haven't been three days of completely dry weather, it's been dry enough.

It's later in the year than the previous two summers we've witnessed, but it's getting done. On Sunday morning Lucas and I take Darcey on the same walk, near the fields we put her on the long lead just in case she's curious about the noises in the field. Upper Field has been cut and it's laying flat for drying, and they're now working in Lower Field. The hay had grown so tall it was falling over on itself, the rain made it weak in places, and the fields looked messy and straggly, but now, cut even if not processed, the field looks like a different place. Expansive, just like the house has felt with the windows open and the air flowing through every room.

Darcey sticks close to us, though her ears perk at the tractor engine, and the voices in the field. But she sticks to our route, and once we're heading upward towards the cabin we take the leash off and she makes a bee line to a shady spot under the cabin where she digs in the sandy soil. If it wasn't for the mosquitoes we'd stay a while, and sit on the cabin porch in the rocking chairs, but the bugs are fierce thanks to the wet summer we've had, and we make our way home, promising ourselves we'll walk the perimeter of the fields more as the rest of the year unfolds.

The new growth on the rhododendrons has turned
from bright spring green to match the deep forest green
of the other leaves. There's a single hydrangea bloom on
the four plants that got hit by the frost, but they're leafy,
reaching toward the sun. The blossoms might still be
coming, but maybe not. Maybe the leaves are where the
energy is heading for this year.

I have plans for the front garden area. In my head,
I can see more wildflowers, and a path leading to the water
spigot, rain barrel, and the oil line. Lucas is dreaming of
a pergola or covered deck type thing. We have rocking
chairs and a bistro set out there now, but the way the sun
hits - it's too much. The direct sun brings on my headaches
and tingly extremities, which plays a part in how I spend
my days during these months. The ocean used to make the
summer bearable. Now, here in the middle of the state, I
have to look closer for things to appreciate in the depths of
summer. The slow movements and days my body craves are
in direct opposition to the do and go and be expectations
we put on these months. I'm finding hibernation in half of
the year, both in the depths of sweat and snow.

It's a quiet Sunday until we start to hear gunshots from across the street where we have new neighbors. It's not a shot here or there, it's over an hour of our otherwise peaceful area sounding like a shooting range. From the window next to my desk I can see them, three or four men standing just beyond the entryway to a clearing, standing in position and firing into the ether. My nervous system starts to go a bit haywire. We're used to a shot ringing out now and then, especially during deer hunting season in the fall, but nothing like this.

By the time we've heard two shots, Darcey becomes frantic. One shot during hunting season will set her off, and this is far too much. We've read that there's a period of time early in a dog's life when you need to introduce all the things, sounds, people, etc., and we know that Darcey missed that window, and fear that she could have some awful memories from her early years that cause her reaction to be quite severe. She tries to fit herself behind my desk, behind the books that line our bookshelves, and behind the entertainment center in the living room. Lucas and I take turns trying to hold her, though she wiggles out of our arms. We give her the medicine that's reserved for times when we know she won't be able to calm down, the downside being it's a twelve-hour dose and she'll be drugged for the rest of the day. Finally, Lucas takes her down to the basement, where there's hardly any way for her to hurt herself while the medicine takes effect. They stay downstairs until I can see the men pack up their guns and bring large cases back to the house.

Even though there are just the regular noises of the day, it takes a long while for her to stop trembling, and even longer for her to stop panting. For a dog that needs a quiet home, one that's worked so hard to get to the point of functioning with daily life, this doesn't feel fair. The questions linger: is this something that will be a regular thing? Is this even allowed? What are we going to do if this is the new normal for a Sunday?

The only answers we have come after searching the local laws, and it sounds like there's nothing stopping our neighbors from firing guns where they were on their property. And even if they had to move a hundred more feet, the sound would still ring out. There's an imbalance of power when there are guns in the mix, and while I try not to stereotype or generalize, it's hard not to.

There's also an attitude about people who move to the state who complain about the way things are - their opinions and complaints are belittled. Our town Facebook page is littered with comments like "You moved to the country, what did you expect?" and there are jokes about people from away who shouldn't be able to vote in local elections. "You moved away from there for a reason, don't bring it with you" is a statement I've heard over and over again, seen on bumper stickers, and overheard at the grocery store. The binary of it all is maddening. It's not a way of thinking that is exclusive to Maine, or our country. It's human to fear the unknown, to dislike and distrust change. While I've accepted that we will always be from "away" no matter how long we've lived here, I'd like to find a way to feel at home not only on my own property, but in my town and state, and on days like today I'm not sure I ever will. It's why we go out back, to the fields. It's why our daily walks are so important, and so grounding. Because we feel at home.

Our reasons for being here seem different than many of those around us - may be in complete contrast. The quiet country life is only as quiet as your neighbors, and right now, our neighbors are shockingly loud in ways that are vastly different from neighbors we've had in the past.

How can we expect the nature that surrounds us to be there, to continue to hold space for us, if we only take from it? Peace, quiet, resources, lives, we take and take. It's one thing to hunt and forage sustainably, but when we step into the fields and forest with only ourselves and our own entertainment in mind, the relationship shifts and the system becomes imbalanced. It becomes less about coexisting with nature and more about imparting our superiority.

Feeling helpless, defeated, and like our senses have been assaulted on so many levels, all we can do is cuddle our sleepy, drugged-up dog, and wait to see what happens.

By the end of the month, the hay has been cut, dried, and baled for the first time this year. There will be a second cutting in September. This first cutting is filled with flowers, heavier, thicker stems, and is high in fiber. This year the field looked more weedy, maybe because it took longer for the conditions of harvesting to be just right, and even then it wasn't perfect. But the second cutting, it's more refined, filled with more protein and less sugar.

This month after some fits and starts, I jumped back into the second draft of my novel. I'm struggling to move through sentences that have gone past flowering and into the weeds, to see the words through a refined lens, to cut back like that second cutting to find a more refined and fleshed out story.

For the first half of the summer, I've been waking up early and getting to my desk before I've fully woken up. I spend two hours on my writing and largely forget about it for the rest of the day. The cost of this is sleepy afternoons, naps before dinner, and an early bedtime. But now, as the weather is finally feeling comfortable in the evenings, I'm finding I want something different.

Maybe some of my struggles with the draft are because I'm not fully awake when I'm working on it, but also I'm forcing my agenda on the work. For years I've held myself back, made my work fit into tiny slots, saying when the kids are older. Now, the kids are older. And yet, I find myself making myself available for their needs like they're still under ten. I say I need to get my work done before they're awake, but why? The demands of teenagers are different than those of smaller children, it's more mental rather than physical. If I add up the hours we're not awake at the same time, it's rather astonishing. And the way I've been crafting my days, the time that we are awake at the same time, I'm exhausted from my early mornings.

There's a shift brewing on the cusp of August. I wonder if the way the weather took its time transitioning from spring to summer has something to do with all of this. Or maybe it's internal and has nothing to do with the seasons of the world, but everything to do with my own becoming. Regardless, changes are being made. The time on my alarm changes, and creeps later and later as the days get closer to the end of the month. The first day that I sleep past six, my body feels rested, and yet not groggy, in a way I haven't felt for a long time. Often I sleep in on the weekends to catch up from the week, but those mornings leave me feeling groggy and slow. In the evenings I'm able to stay up later with Lucas and the kids, and while we're just watching television or reading in bed, there's a closeness I miss when my schedule is so far from theirs. While I don't want to go so far as saying I need to fully embrace my teenagers' schedules - sleeping until noon doesn't appeal to me in any way these days - I think a shift towards a less extreme schedule is what August, and my body, calls for. Oftentimes I forget that I can create my own schedule, and while sometimes it needs to work around the school system, our unscheduled days of the coming month are open for interpretation. They're open to a different way of being.

Near the end of the month Paige and I drive over to the White Mountains in New Hampshire to visit friends who are there for a family camping trip. We visit Lower Falls in Conway, and my friend Kylee and I spend a few hours wading in the cold mountain water that flowed over the falls, away from the strong current, while our kids go between splashing and sunbathing. We talk about both of our work, she's a holistic healer who is inherently creative. I share about the struggles I've been having getting into my second draft, but also the way I feel like I haven't embraced my creative work as fully mine. I keep looking for someone to tell me this is the right work for me.

Kylee asks a question that feels familiar, and I know it has come up with other writers, but I haven't focused the question on myself, ever.

"What if you let your writing nurture you?"

My initial response is that it's a lot of pressure to put on my writing. I don't want my writing to have to sustain me. But that's not what she's asking. Something that nurtures us doesn't necessarily have the same pressure to sustain us. There's something here, something that I want to dig into and question more.

What does it mean to let something be nurturing?

And when I really think about it, really look hard,

why wouldn't we want our work to also nurture us in a way? And if you're lucky enough for your work to be your passion, as writing is for me, why not embrace that side of it?

What I realize is that I haven't wanted to put any expectations on my writing, but maybe in being careful not to do so, I've held it at a distance. I haven't wanted to let myself get too close to embracing my writing life fully, because I'm scared. I've held it at arms length because it's something that I want, deeply, and I'm afraid that I am not up for the challenges that come with the writing life - the rejection, the work, the creativity, the problem-solving, all of it.

The definition of nurture, as a verb, is to care for and encourage the growth or development of.

What if my writing encouraged my growth and development as a writer and a person? Isn't that the way it works, naturally?

These are all questions I take with me and ponder long after we've left the waterfalls behind, hours after we hug Kylee and her girls goodbye and go our separate ways. They stick with me as I open up various files on my computer, and look at the words I've written with a tender, soft gaze, meeting them where I'm at, and where they are at. The questions swirl in my head round and round like the water that cascaded over the falls and into pools where the current pulled and mixed and then eventually stilled. And the ultimate question, "What if you let your work nurture you?" combined with the concept of stepping into my own story from earlier in the month, they follow me from July into August, and it feels like another layer of self has been discovered, another level unearthed.

The final days of July are dotted with sweet gifts. One day my father leaves a cucumber from the garden and an Echinacea flower on our doorstep. Another day brings half the potato harvest to my kitchen counter. Paige's smile and contentment with completing a bedroom makeover, turning the previous bright yellow room into a dreamy dark green sanctuary of music and art, hinting at a fairytale existence. Evenings where the mist hangs in the fields. Photos are shared of a fawn checking out the lavender patch over by the meadow. Listening to Fynn play bass at the local farmer's market, taking steps to turn a dream into reality.

And the last parting gifts of July come in the form

of two days where the temperature barely hits 70 degrees. Outside, cool breezes envelop us and keep the bugs at bay while the summer sun still warms our backs as we walk the newly cut fields. Inside the windows are open and we hold our breath on the last Sunday of the month in case our neighbors decide to take it upon themselves to dot the day with their recreational activities. But as the day unfolds, we exhale into the fresh air that swirls around us, filling each corner of the house, and expanding through our property and beyond. If this is what the rest of the summer has in mind, we'll gladly accept it with open arms.

August

On the first of the month there are blue skies mixed with puffy white clouds. The temperatures stay in the seventies, the breeze is cool with hints of the coming season.

Earlier in the week I caught wind that pick-your-own blueberries were on sale at our local orchard, Ricker Hill, where there are a few rows of blueberry bushes nestled in with their many varieties of apples.

Berry picking, blueberry in particular, has been a staple in our summers for as long as I can remember. We have pictures of Fynn toddling around carrying a green cardboard pint container, a one-year-old Paige strapped on my back in a carrier reaching for a berry I passed back to her. I can remember the outfit she wore, the tiny shorts and the sweet top with flutter sleeves, the bucket hat Fynn wore with the orange stripe. Years ago the kids visited their grandparents in New Hampshire, where Ted and Mary Lou made picker buckets for them using plastic cups with strings tied to them, the cups hung around their necks and the blueberries went plunk plunk plunk as they were dropped. Little hands were stained blue by tiny wild berries, and later Grandma made muffins were devoured by even the pickiest eaters.

Somehow we missed blueberry picking last year. Some years are like that. This year, other things are going to the wayside in the name of schedules and shifting priorities and seasonal anomalies. Such is the way when you're witnessing the growth of humans happening in a heartbeat, and that heartbeat speeds with unanswered questions and endless possibilities.

But blueberries feel like a priority at this moment. The air turned cool as the month rolled over into August, and space opened up for an hour or so to spend with my kids, and so we drive the ten minutes down the road and up the hill and through the family homes that the Ricker's still inhabit, and find ourselves mostly in quiet companionship, togetherness in a way that feels comfortable and known, familiar.

We catch glimpses of the fall harvest already

ripening in the early Autumn sun, and between the surprisingly cool fresh air, the views of the mountains, and the pleasant company of the teens, my heart feels as full and content as the memories of other days spent picking are vivid. The layers of the natural world mixed with the layers of our togetherness form a picture fit for a frame, or at least another snapshot embedded in my bank of core memories.

As with every stage of this parenting and living journey, I have one foot dipping out and back in a circular pattern around the other foot which is planted firmly in the present. The moving foot dances to the future, back to the past, visiting other lives. The magic comes when it stands next to the other, breathing heavily with knowledge and memories of it all, the steady foot grounding them both, embodying the moment and all it holds.

Between the three of us, we pick twenty pounds of berries, all headed for pies and cakes, containers in the fridge for snacking and topping granola, and the freezer to dot our winter with the sweetness of summer.

Slowly, the humidity creeps back in to remind us that autumn is still a ways away. We close the windows and close ourselves off from the natural world, so we think. But early one morning I'm in the sitting room with my tea and journal, and a scratching sound comes from the fireplace. I look in, but see nothing, and go about my morning. An hour or so later Fynn is sitting in the same place, I'm busying myself in the kitchen before a video call with a friend, making another cup of tea and putting away breakfast dishes.

Fynn says, slow and steady but with a slight alarm in his voice, "Uh, Mom? There's a bird in the fireplace."

I look through the glass pane and see a small sparrow, covered in ashes and soot. It jumps from place to place, kicking up more ashes with its wings at every turn. We call for Lucas, and he comes in with a garbage bag. At first we try to cover the door with the bag, and then open it to see if the bird will fly in on its own. It doesn't. So Lucas asks Fynn for duct tape, and then he covers the opening with the bag, taping the sides and top to the fireplace, and rips the bottom of the bag open. The bird is sitting on a brick in the back, still and quiet as we prepare, probably scared out of its poor mind. Next, with myself and Fynn watching over his shoulder, Lucas reaches in with the bag and manages to scoop the bird into the plastic, quickly and carefully taking the bag off the fireplace, and carries the bird outside. Unceremoniously he lets it fly out into the air, asking it not to come back through the chimney.

Inside you'd never know anything happened. There's not a speck of ash on the floor, nothing spilled out from the fireplace.

But there's a shift in the air. An energy. When a wild thing comes indoors, it's unsettling. It makes me wonder what the wild things think about us coming outdoors. The separation, human made of course, between wild and tame, what belongs indoors and out, notions of safety and comfort, they all play on my mind as the day goes on. And as ever, I try to connect and give meaning to events, and the bird in the fireplace gets tucked into memory to revisit another day.

The sixth of August holds two anniversaries: Lucas and my wedding anniversary, and the anniversary of the closing date of the homestead. This year it's our 18th and second anniversaries. The eighteen years have gone by in a blink, and the last two in particular at warp speed. Two years ago when we were asked if we had a preference for a closing date, we decided a Friday would work well, and it just happened to be the day we got married. When we realized that, I just figured it would make it easy to remember both dates. I didn't think about them forever being intertwined.

This year the sixth falls on a Sunday with clear weather, and we've decided to celebrate with lunch out on my parents porch and an afternoon of croquet. My father has mowed a bit of yarn down extra, creating a court of sorts, and after lunch pickets are placed in formation, colors of matching mallets and balls are chosen. This year our wedding anniversary is mentioned more than the property. I don't ever remember my parents celebrating a closing date anniversary, but then, growing up we never lived in one place for more than a few years, there was never an intention of a forever home. Here, it's more than just a house. It's the anniversary of a wild dream come to life, and if not a forever home - it's a for the very long future home.

After one game we come back to the porch and sit with cake and glasses of ice water. Fynn sits quietly across the table from me, and then he points out - in that same slow and slightly alarmed voice he used when the bird was in the fireplace - that there's a groundhog in the garden. Expletives are voiced by our master gardener, and as my father starts walking towards the garden looking like Mr.

McGregor with his hat and beard, Mom starts putting two and two together about just who has been snacking on their garden. The groundhog makes its way into the compost bin for safety, and then in what appears to be a bit of a standoff between him and Dad, he runs away into the back meadow, leaving questions of where he came from and how have we not seen him before.

Throughout, Darcey sits at our feet, unbothered by the little critter causing a bit of chaos in the garden.

Animal sightings tend to bring a little bit of levity and wonder to the moment, no matter if they're destructive or benign. Like the sparrow in the fireplace, these moments remind us we're not alone.

As I embark on a month of novel revision, I have a conversation with my friend Michelle who is a writer visiting the states from Rome, and when discussing the need for breaks, we stumble upon the notion that maybe it's not the writing we get burned out from. Maybe it's all the things around it. As writers, we don't actually turn off our writing brains. We are constantly writing in our heads, narrating our days, pulling phrases out of thin air and grasping onto them until we can find a pen and paper or a notes app on our phones. Maybe the burnout we feel comes from expectations we're beholden to in our everyday lives, not from the stories themselves, the words that live within us that are always finding a way out.

Another group of writer friends who chat regularly often end up referring to things each of us comes back to or says regularly. One of the things I say that gets brought up again and again is that writing looks like life.

The question from last month about what it would look like if I let my writing nurture me is at the forefront of my mind as I weave revision of the novel into my days. I come to the pages with an awareness of this being my work. Doubts arise, as they always do, but somehow at this point in my writing life I've gained the knowledge and trust that if I sit with the doubt, if I sit with the voices that are telling me to find another job, that this isn't work I'm cut out for, they dissipate. What's left is the understanding that this is the work I am not only cut out for, but want to do, with all of my heart.

One thing I've learned this year in particular is that if I get stuck, I need to ground myself. For certain writing it's by getting outside for a walk, to let my feet touch the literal ground and let my senses experience my subject matter. The novel I'm working on takes place at a yarn shop, and so when an issue comes up that needs more thinking, more unpacking, I reach for my knitting and knit a round or two of a sweater that I've recently started. It's enough to keep me in the story, but also let my mind wander intentionally. The feel of the yarn does what the birdsong does on the trail, it brings me into the present moment - my present moment - and ties me to the story that's unfolding in front of me. We are linked to the stories we write, fiction and nonfiction, by so much more than words.

I'm standing in the kitchen on the evening of August eighth, finishing up the dinner dishes. There's a dish towel in one hand, a roasting pan in the other, when a rumble echoes through the house, and I feel an unsteadiness from within. Lucas goes downstairs to check on the furnace, I call my parents to see if they have power, as another possibility is that a transistor somewhere nearby blew. Mom answers and has all the same questions for me, and they're echoed by Dad over speaker phone. With no more answers than we started with, we all promise to investigate and let each other know if we find out anything. Minutes later my father calls back, letting me know he spoke with a neighbor down the road who heard and felt the same thing. Later that night we find out there was an Earthquake, 2.5 at 6:04pm about twenty miles away. Close enough to be heard and felt. Close enough to make us wonder what else the earth has in store for us.

The weather dips in and out of rainy, humid days, and when we land on one filled with sunshine we all get into the car and head to the coast to introduce Lucas to Wolf's Neck Park. We pack a simple lunch of sandwiches, water bottles, and swimsuits. I bring my knitting. The park is busier than it was when the kids and I visited in June, and there's a half a dozen artists set up with easels and canvases. Families all clad in hiking boots explore the trails and rocky coastline, but we make a bee line to an open spot on the rocky shore that butts up against a boulder and some shade and we spread our quilt over ocean softened pebbles and set up camp.

There is no one in the water, the bay isn't the sandy shoreline you'd want for wading. But nonetheless Lucas and I make our way to the water, leaving the kids at the blankets, one to take a nap, the other to climb a tree to find a perfect reading spot. Our feet get sucked into the clay and silt of the bay floor, it's slippery underfoot, and our steps are intentional. Across the way we watch Osprey soar overhead and land on nests. We take small step after step, trying to watch out for crabs and the occasional rock. Finally knee deep, I lean back and let my body fall into the water. It's August, and the water does not take my breath away with its chill, but it lingers on my lips like from an extra salty potato chip. We slowly make our way back to the blanket where we dry off. I reach for my knitting, the same project that grounds me in revision grounds me here, too.

Earlier in the month my mind started drifting to an upcoming international trip, and what I'd pack for it. I convinced myself that I needed a work horse of a sweater, a simple one that could go with any outfit, and weather any storm. I had just the yarn for just that type of project in my stash, and so I cast on a simple raglan sweater in an undyed yarn, Cascade Eco Wool in a medium weight. When I knit, I think about what the trip will entail, what I'll need. And when I find myself in the midst of a wardrobe crisis of self, I remember I do one thing well: knitwear. I lean into that, just as I did in the winter when I wasn't sure how to dress myself. I start there, and in my mind I build a vacation wardrobe based off the sweater that comes together in my hands.

While we sit at the coast with salt crusted limbs and lips, yarn moving between my fingers, the weight of the sweater growing with each stitch, I think about the trip. I think about what it'll be like to spend two and a half weeks in the beginning of my favorite season - autumn - away from home. When the thoughts start to be too much, the unknowns and the worries that come up before any travel, I take a deep breath, look out at the water, feel the rocks under my feet, and know that it'll all be okay. I don't know how, but I know that because I've woven slices of heaven, the rocky shoreline, my writing desk and my words, and my comfortable knitting chair in the living room, all into this sweater, I'll be able to take the comforts and the joys of who and where I've come from wherever I wear the sweater.

With the wardrobe conundrum still in mind, one night while I'm knitting I order new shoes, socks, a backpack, and a pair of jeans for the trip. For the rest of the month I alternate between breaking in a pair of sneakers and a pair of ballet flats. On a day trip with Paige, I use the backpack instead of my purse, and I feel a sense of lightness with both hands free, not worrying about a bag swinging from my arm. This is the bit of travel that we don't often talk about, how in preparing for trips, grand or small, we prepare to be ourselves out in the world. We prepare for how we want to show up for and as ourselves. I take this opportunity to reevaluate my wardrobe, but also to reevaluate how I care for myself when I am not home. Comfort reigns supreme, and so I go with a backpack instead of a tote bag. I take the time to break in the shoes instead of leaving it for the last minute. I knit a sweater that I know will bring me comfort on this grand solo adventure. While I think about being away from my husband and kids - and Darcey - the longest I've ever been away, instead of wallowing in worry, I'm being proactive in a way that comes from knowing myself, knowing my needs, it comes from listening.

I can't help but think the months spent with daily walks in the woods, the quiet that comes with early mornings spent writing and thinking, lingering over words and dreams, all informs this way of being. Where in the past I may not have been willing to take the time to listen, spending more time listening to the music of the fields and forest has given way to a path towards myself.

One night we spend the evening at the firepit by the cabin with Mom and Dad, it's the first time using the fire pit since Toby and Adrienne were here in the winter. Every time we passed by the firepit, we looked at it and said, soon. But on this particular evening I get a text from Dad saying they'll be out there if we'd like to join them. There's a giant tree stump in the firepit, pulled from somewhere on the property, and tonight is the night we're going to burn it. The mosquitoes are fierce, and we're all doused in so much bug spray we must be flammable, but we persevere for a while. Bats fly overhead, and we urge them to make a meal out of every mosquito we bat from our exposed skin. The smoke touches each person in turn. We drink hot tea and cocoa, and indulge in marshmallows. The night grows late and when Darcey and I make our way home the kids follow in turn, but Lucas stays out with my parents. They wait until past midnight as the fire burns out. He comes to bed smelling like a campfire, and sighs with content as he falls asleep next to me.

Starting a third of the way through the month, there's a bubbling sense of dread that's starting to churn in my stomach. It quiets down here and there, but it's constant. On a Monday it overwhelms during a day when nothing seems to go right. I can't find my footing through the quicksand of the day, can't even manage a smile at the dog. Eventually we make our way outside for a walk, I try to take photos but they all feel flat. The farmer from down the road has cut the hay around the houses, and the landscape changed considerably. Where there was depth, where there was interest, it's all just a line of property. The tree lines stop your eyes, but the boulders and trees that dot the expanse get lost.

We keep walking. The larger fields are starting to grow back just a bit from their cutting, and the fields are a vibrant green. The expansiveness in these fields play tricks on the eyes, too. Only when we're on Chickadee Lane, surrounded by trees and bushes, do I find myself exhaling, and then inhaling fully. The openness of the fields is too much, leaving me feeling too vulnerable. But here, with trees at my sides and overhead, it feels safe. The green is lush, an oddity for August, but with the weather patterns it's to be expected this year. Nonetheless it's a welcome surprise to find such a variety of green in one place during the depths of summer.

One afternoon Paige and I decide at the last minute to go to the same lake I went to last month by myself for a quick dip. When we leave the house the sky is clear aside from a few stray clouds. Twenty minutes down the road, as soon as we step out of the car we hear the far off rumble of thunder. We look at each other, both our sets of eyebrows raised.

"Do you want to leave?" she asks me.

I look at the sky, there's dark clouds in the distance.

"Let's just dip in and out," I tell her. She looks at me in surprise. I'm an overly cautious person, and I'm sure she remembers all of the times we were at the coast on the beach and packed up as soon as the sky even hinted at thunder.

But here, it's just us, our towels, and the lake.

There's barely anyone here, just a few people

at either end of the small stretch of sand. We throw our clothes down with the towels, and wade out. I fall back in the water, submerging my entire body. It wasn't so long ago that Paige was the first one in, always ducking under the water, our little fish. Now, she is careful not to dive in as she has on a full face of makeup. Instead, she wades in, her arms out straight from her sides, her fingers dance along the top of the water like a water strider. In front of us the mountains loom, the sky still blue and bright. Behind us the sky turns a darker shade of gray, and after two more rolls of thunder we make a mad, wet, dash to the car, laughing the whole way.

There is no rain on the ride home. At the homestead the sky's still blue, and they haven't heard any thunder. The storm stays away from our little plot of land, and if we hadn't witnessed it ourselves we might never have known it happened.

In a blink it's the middle of August, Paige has turned fifteen. We celebrate with a lunch out in Portland with Mary Lou and Ted. The city is about halfway between us, and Paige picks a hibachi restaurant where there's a gazillion options and everyone can find something they like to eat. We've always tried to include grandparents in celebrations, and while we can count the number of friend parties the kids have had on one hand, their birthdays have always been filled with family - though we have a relatively small one - and love. All too soon our meal is finished, and we're packing up, saying goodbye at the car where hugs are dispersed and Lucas promises we'll see them again soon.

On the way home, our bellies full of sushi and teriyaki, we run into trouble. Two minutes from home, we find that we can't get to our house via roads. There's been an accident in town, and the road we normally take is blocked by the emergency helicopter, and the alternate road we could take is blocked by the accident. We've been gone for hours, the animals need tending, and we're ready to be home. I'm on the phone with my parents to see if there's traffic moving in front of our house, when Lucas puts the car into park and steps out onto the road. There's an access path from this one to our fields belonging to the farmer who hays for us. It's roped off, but Lucas unhooks the barrier, comes back to the car, gets us out of the line of traffic and we take the very back way home. We drive along the river for a moment, and then through a heavily wooded bit that opens up into Lower Field. We go slowly, carefully.

211

There's been so much rainfall, but the ground holds and our Subaru is solid and steady, and we witness the fields from a different vantage point. It moves quickly, and looks so small compared to when you're walking the perimeter, or standing in the middle of the field.

In a few moments, we're home, and half an hour later we hear the helicopter depart.

Knowing these very back ways home, knowing where the land connects, knowing it's safe to use a neighbors access road, it's like we unlocked another level of belonging.

August rolls along at a slow and steady pace. I work diligently on my second draft, and find a rhythm that comes naturally. There's a steadiness to the month that sets the tone for a transition into autumn.

On our morning walk we catch a glimpse of a ghost pipe, an ethereal plant that does not contain chlorophyll. While it's often mistaken for mushrooms, it feeds off of fungi that is somehow connected to trees, indirectly feeding off of the tree. It blooms only one week of the year, but witnessing its ghostly stems and blooms before and after also feels like a privilege and a treasure.

Further on our walk there are sprinkles of yellow mixed in with the otherwise green leaves of the entryway up to Hobbit Hill. On Chickadee Lane there's a lone red leaf on the path.

On an evening walk we see three deer, two in Lower Field, one in Upper. They graze, without paying us any attention. Another evening walk during the golden hour, there are dozens of dragonflies flying around the top of Hobbit Hill. It brings smiles to our faces that linger as Paige, Lucas, Darcey, and I make our way up the cabin steps and look out at the fields that hum, as if electric with the insects, and the true golden glow of the light leaves me with a feeling of comfort and ease. At home I know I'll turn the kettle on, look fondly at the echinacea flowers gathered in a vase on the windowsill, and settle into a comfy chair with my knitting and a cup of tea, but here, I wrap my arms around Paige and lean on her shoulder, not wishing to be anyplace else.

I'd set myself the goal of finishing the second draft of my novel by September. Surprising myself, it's complete with over a week to spare. I save it as a PDF, and send it over to my first reader, Lucas. He's been my biggest champion, and is an honest and thoughtful reader who asks the right kind of questions and holds the creative process with a tenderness writers long for in their readers. Sending your work out to be read in any stage is frightening in ways, but especially early on. My hope is he'll have time to read it when I'm away next month. There's nothing more nerve wracking than being in the same house, let alone the same room, as someone who is reading your work. The challenge is in letting them have their experience with your words without butting in to ask what point they're at in any given moment, and not reading a world into an innocent comment. It's best if I'm as far away as possible, and being across the Atlantic while he's reading my novel feels appropriate in a way that I find comical but also true.

My friend Jess is a fellow Maine knitter. I met her through Instagram years ago when connected over knitting, and she was one of the first people to reach out to me to ask if we could connect in person after our move north. We started meeting at a local yarn shop's knitting afternoon, and we've ended up as confidants and friends who have more in common than we could have initially thought. Our friendship has evolved organically and is one of the few local connections I've made since becoming a Maine Resident. It hasn't been easy connecting with others here. Maybe because we don't live in a neighborhood, or because we don't use the public schools, or - as I often wonder late at night - maybe it's just me.

But the thing is when I'm with Jess or the few close friends who know my heart and connect over things we're all passionate about and bring curiosity, heart listening, and compassion to conversations, I don't think I'm the cause, the problem. I think finding friendship midway through life when there are so many things pulling at you is difficult. Moreso, I think treasuring the ones you've cultivated, remembering it's about quality over quantity, is the key.

A few weeks ago, Jess asked if I'd accompany her on a leg of the Maine Yarn Cruise, an annual event shops in Maine participate in where there's a passport you get stamped at each location, drawings for yarny gifts, and anyone who visits all of the locations is entered to win a giant prize. While I'm not participating in the yarn cruise this year - I did last year and my yarn budget hasn't recovered since - I say yes, and we leave on a rainy Friday.

The rain continues all day, from Bangor where we stop at One Lupine, picking up a hand thrown mug with lupine's on it and some yarn in a colorway named after the same flower, to Calais near the Canadian border, to Machias where we dine at a restaurant looking over a drizzly marsh.

The next day we start off at Western Head Preserve in Cutler, and it's still drizzling. On the way to the walk we pass a deer we think is a decoy laying down in the grass. Jess yells out the car window, "Are you real?" It doesn't blink, but it's ear twitches. We fall over ourselves in a fit of laughter. Next on our route is Hancock, Southwest Harbor on Mount Desert Island, Castine, and down the coast to Belfast and finally to Camden. By the time we're in Castine the sky is blue and the temperatures are on the rise. After our final stop we have dinner in Camden, looking out over a harbor and the coast. Seeing as many yarn stores as we have in the last twenty four hours, they blend together, and we spend our meal trying to recap and recall everything that we've seen and done. It blurs together, just like the trip to Asheville with Gina and Allison did. The time away, untethered except to the bonds of friendship, speeds past in a way that lingering in the woods never does.

I get home with just enough time to catch up with

Lucas and the kids briefly, before falling into bed. At dinner they tell me about their day spent with Mary Lou and Ted down at the condo. After the kids go upstairs, Lucas tells me that his father's health has been rough this week, that he's concerned. Ted has dementia and PTSD from his service in the Vietnam War, and the challenges of his health are becoming more obvious and concerning as time goes on. This age we're at is one that author Kelly Corrigan wrote an entire book about, called *The Middle Place*. In it, she writes about her journey of being in the stage of ushering teenagers into adulthood while walking alongside aging parents whose needs and the dynamics of the relationship they have with you are changing.

It's a stage neither of us nor our parents would want to admit we're in, but here we are. We try to ask questions without being intrusive, take their answers at face value, knowing there are probably depths they don't want to burden us with. At some point we'll all dive in, but we've only waded into the shallow end thus far.

With heavy hearts we go to bed, and at 2:30am we get a phone call that changes everything, and sends us into the deep end.

Mary Lou's voice comes through the phone in the darkness of our bedroom to tell us that Ted has just been taken to the emergency room, his health took a drastic turn over the last few hours. She asks us to come in the morning, and we say we'll try to get some sleep, but instead Lucas and I cling to each other in the dark, not knowing or wanting to face what the next day will bring.

Sunday is spent in the waiting room at the hospital, as only one of us is allowed back with Ted in the ER until he's sent up to a room. At the end of the day, no closer to having our questions answered, and with no plan of Ted being able to leave, Lucas wants and needs to stay close so I leave him with his parents. That night Lucas and Mary Lou say goodbye to Ted for the evening while he's coherent and eating dinner. The next morning they find out he took another turn, and has been sedated. Thus starts a cycle that none of us fully understand or want for him. The next few days are spent waiting, asking questions, more waiting and searching for answers. There are countless texts and phone calls and long days and even longer nights praying for him to become conscious in a way that is safe for him and those around him.

On Wednesday when Mary Lou and I are on the way to see Ted, it rains our entire drive from the condo to the hospital. At points it downpours, and I white knuckle it all the way up the highway to the exit, aware of Mary Lou's presence in the passenger seat, her hands tucked neatly in her lap, her gaze straight ahead. Shortly after we get to the hospital the rain stops for the rest of the day. But as soon as we get into the car to head home around dinner time, it started raining again, turning to downpours once more on the highway. After I drop Mary Lou off and head back to the homestead that night there's a rainbow just south of Portland. Further down the road a red tailed hawk takes flight and follows alongside the car, ushering me home.

Off the highway in Poland, I pass two deer on the side of the road, and it feels like I catch one's eye out the passenger window. It watches, and then out the rear view mirror, I can see it looking both ways before it and its companion cross the road. That split second looking into its deep, dark eyes is enough to unlock the emotions I've held tight since the wee hours of Sunday morning.

September

The beginning of the month comes and goes without much notice of the date or even days of the week let alone the weather. At home we walk around in a fog, waiting for phone calls and texts with news. Rarely are Lucas and I in the same place at the same time. We shuffle between the hospital with Mary Lou and Ted, and at home with the kids. Only a few days into the month, over Labor Day weekend, the heartbreaking decision to move Ted to a local hospice house is made after days of prayer and unresponsiveness. The battles he's fighting are set aside, and he's able to rest. Just over twenty-four hours later, way sooner than anyone anticipates, he passes peacefully from this world to the next.

The following day I take the kids down to Wells to be with Lucas and Mary Lou. At the condo, where we've spent weekends and vacations and hours playing Uno and watching movies and sharing meals, Paige and I make dinner. While waiting for the oven to preheat we sit with our legs stretched out across the kitchen floor. Her eyes well up and she says, "It feels like someone is missing." I nod in understanding.

At dinner, no one sits in Ted's seat.

When I finally open my journal, I realize I haven't written a single word in it since the day I left for the yarn cruise trip with Jess. Though I've been writing almost nonstop in my head, processing things through words, none have made it to the page.

When we were at the hospital and then later at the hospice house, my knitting was a constant companion. My fingers needed to move, my brain couldn't concentrate on a book through the ever-constant beeps of hospital monitors and the comings and goings of nursing staff and visitors. At home I picked up my knitting as well, the hours of being at home were long and anxious, waiting for news, but my fingers flew. By the time Ted was moved to the hospice home and we knew all our plans for the rest of the month would shift, I'd completed two smaller projects and brought along the sweater I was working on for my trip. The body was done, and I was on the first sleeve.

Not even a week later, after a day of feeling all the stages of grief in one, I finish the sweater. The weight of it feels like a hug, the style of it - simple and sturdy - reminds me of Ted. The adventures it's seen and will see are different than I anticipated. But knit into it are moments of peace at the coast, and prayers and memories of Ted, specifically with his grandchildren, while at the hospice house. With each garment I knit I hope to remember what I went through while knitting it, what the circumstances were surrounding the knit, and what life events happened. Sometimes the stories stick with me, like with the shawl I knit half in our old home, half in our current one, or the sweater that I just couldn't get right before we moved, and had to start over a handful of times only for it to go smoothly from cast on to finished garment while living in Maine. But for others, the stories fade and the memories associated with the sweaters are ones that happen while wearing them.

This sweater, though, is one that will hold memories of its making, and fond memories of Ted, for years to come.

Lucas joins Mary Lou on a trip to Florida to gather a few items before the funeral. The kids and I are back at home, spending many hours together but also separately, finding our way after such a loss. After knitting furiously for days, my hands need a rest, but my brain doesn't know where to land. I think about writing, but everything seems trivial. At the same time, I'm drawn to my Kindle, where there are a half dozen or so novels waiting for me. They're light and fluffy, the kind that got me through the early days of the Pandemic when there was so much uncertainty. I find myself wondering how I could write anything, especially things that aren't heavy, but somewhere in my mind I can recognize the value in stories that are pure enjoyment, for many reasons. It reminds me of how Lucas read my second draft while in the hospital at his dad's side. The novel's subject matter touches somewhat close to home, so I told him he didn't have to read it, especially not just then. He looked over and smiled a tired smile, saying he'd put it down if it got to be too much. Over the next few days, he'd text me or bring up the book over the phone when we weren't together, letting me know where he was, a few of his "I knew it!" moments and overall comments. The book gave us something to focus on, to touch base about, other than the stress and grief at hand. It brought a few moments of levity to our days, as well as a sense of connection that felt like a touchstone during a tumultuous time when it felt like we were oceans away from one another.

For a while, the only time the kids and I spend outside is during Darcey's daily walk. The mosquitoes and the humidity have made it so that we are outdoors only as much as is purely necessary. While Lucas is away, Darcey and I find our way back to routines after a few weeks of unknowns. For the most part, there is always someone home with Darcey, and the last two weeks have left her a bit out of sorts. Our daily rhythms have been upended, but again, we find our way back to them.

Even still, the morning walks feel hurried. One morning I'm struck by raindrops on blades of grass, how surface tension is at play. I linger over the Goldenrod hanging heavy with rain and humidity and then stop for a moment to marvel over a dozen mushrooms that sprung up on Chickadee Lane seemingly overnight. But my marveling is short-lived as the second I crouch down there's a buzz in my ear, and I can feel little creatures landing on bug spray-soaked exposed skin.

I'm craving quiet, slow time spent outdoors, and it feels like the outdoors is pushing me away at every turn.

On the 15th, the day I had originally planned to head across the Atlantic, we're preparing for Ted's funeral. There are shirts to launder and iron, outfits to try on, and ties to practice tying. Hurricane Lee is coming up the coast, extended family members are down with Covid, and a slew of unknowns arise as we walk through the day before the funeral.

Amid chores and my to-do list, Darcey and I go out for a walk. The weather has shifted, and the mosquitoes are kept at bay by the cooler temperatures and gentle breeze. This is Darcey weather, and frankly, my weather as well, and she runs ahead and then doubles back to me, her tongue lolling out of one side of a grin. We take a longer trek than we have in the past few months, extending our walk down to the fields and up to the cabin. The seasonal change is imminent, if not slower this year. Or maybe it's that time is moving strangely.

The hurricane is set to bring tropical storm conditions throughout Maine, and even though we're far from the coast, we brace for wind and rain all the same. We pull in the loose furniture, next door they're securing tomato plants. We go through the movements of preparation because otherwise, our minds will overwhelm us. Action first. Emotions later.

The morning of the funeral we all wake up on time. We move around each other as we get ready for the day, Darcey sits in her safe spot underneath the dining room table which is at the heart of the house, watching us move in and out of rooms. Paige helps me with my makeup, I can hear Lucas teaching Fynn how to put on a tie. Lucas wears his kilt made up of the family tartan, and dawns his father's sporran, as well as his sgian dubh, a knife one wears in kilt socks. He explains that if you wear it as he is, with it showing, it means you come in peace. Hidden, it means the opposite.

We're on a sort of autopilot, but not. During the hour-and-a-half drive to the church my knitting sits in a bag at my feet, I don't pick it up once. The car is quiet, and the

kids are in the backseat, both with headphones on. Every
once and a while Lucas moves his hand towards mine, or
I reach for him. We stop at a rest area on the highway, and
we both smile about being the most well-dressed visitors.
Back in the car, Fynn asks if Lucas got any funny looks
because of his kilt, we both say we didn't notice. And I
didn't. I only saw the most handsome man I've ever seen,
filled with grief, standing tall, doing his father proud.

We muddle through the rest of the day, and are left
with core memories. Familiar faces and embraces, Ted's
casket draped in the American flag, in the background
of every moment. He was like that in life, present and
watchful. Mary Lou reads a poem he wrote to her from
Vietnam. Lucas reads words he wrote about his father, his
voice shakes with emotion and steadies with affection.
Paige wears pins that remind her of her grandfather, Winnie
the Pooh and Dumbo. Watching the three grandchildren
together, all dawned in black. Flowers, so many flowers.
Fynn and Lucas and my own father as pallbearers, Fynn
wearing aviator sunglasses that are similar to the ones
Ted always wore. The way the hurricane stepped aside in

favor of sunshine, winds swirling around us as Taps rang out at the cemetery. An officer presents Mary Lou with the flag. Looking over to see my mother's tearful face. Paige and I embrace as Lucas touches the casket, I reach past her towards Fynn and he steps in to join us. The feeling of driving away from Ted, where he now rests overlooking the ocean at the cemetery. And eventually, later that night, the feeling of being bone tired, and the relief of coming home.

Even with the funeral behind us, the fog continues. Lucas comes down with a cold, my throat feels one coming but it doesn't come to fruition. Somewhere along the lines the humidity leaves and the weather lines up with the calendar and once again we're welcomed outside. We start our homeschooling year, I fill to-do's on a blank planner for the kids, and Friday night dinners resume.

Historically, September is one of my slowest months writing-wise. I remember lamenting last year about how this always happens, how I shove my writing aside as my brain can't handle writing and homeschooling all at once. It's not true for the remainder of the school year, but at first, it's a lot. This year instead of fighting it, I'm embracing the need for the scales to tip in favor of homeschooling, knowing they'll return to balance in a week or two once our rhythms really start to establish themselves, and I can carve out my regular writing time once again. At this point, it's a matter of not necessarily finding the time for writing, but more so it feels like I've thrown a handful of activities up in the air, and I'm waiting to see where they fall into place.

I know there's time for writing, there always is. Even when I think there isn't, there is. But I also know that it's challenging for me to sit down and write when there are loads of loose ends in the day. The amount of time I'm needed as a mom, and homeschool parent specifically, shifts depending on the subjects we're on each day, the way hormones are playing out, and just the general ebb and flow of life with teenagers. Throw in a side of grief and a handful of new experiences, and it feels like I'm on call more often than not. But, I know things will settle down.

Algebra Two, Geometry, Geology, Organic Chem, History, Language... There's familiarity in the rhythms and it's something we all are looking for in theory.

But in practice it is another story.

Monday starts off before I've fully woken up, one kid is ready to start on their school work before the time I said I'd be ready, and instead of welcoming and encouraging the self-start, I have to get over myself and my annoyance. Truthfully, she doesn't need my help to get started, but my expectation was to mark the beginning of the school year in a special way. Once again, I have to remember in years past that never went well. The kids don't want ceremony, they don't want to commemorate, they want to get started and dig in, knowing that there's work to be done, work to finish so they can get to the other side of the day and relax.

Tuesday is much of the same, except I know to stay out of the way and simply be there when needed, to ask the right question at the right time, when to start conversations, and when to leave well enough alone.

On Wednesdays Fynn has an outdoor adventure club he participates in, where he spends one afternoon a week in community with other homeschooled teenagers finding different places along the coast of Maine to explore and learn new skills. We drop him off an hour away from home, and it makes no sense to double back and then do the same drive only two hours later, so Paige and I decree

Wednesdays our Adventure Day. Today, I don't really tell Paige what we're doing, until right before we do it. I offer up the bookstore, her favorite place in Portland, and her eyes grow wide. From there, the offer of Trader Joe's to grab an easy lunch and stock up on autumn favorites delights her. And then, when I suggest driving out to Mackworth Island, I can see a sparkle in her eyes, and she doesn't hesitate to say yes.

The whole day has felt more like getting back to routine than the first part of the week. This adventuring is what I used to do with the kids almost daily. When they were little and we lived in a tiny apartment, I'd pack a bag and secure them in their car seats in our old Volvo wagon, and we'd head out to playgrounds, nature trails, museums, Ted and Mary Lou's when they lived in New Hampshire on the side of a mountain, or even up to see my brother when he was still stateside. My favorite was always those crisp autumn mornings when the kids would need their sweet little knit hats, layered up in long-sleeve tees and soft-as-cloud hooded sweatshirts. I'd grab a latte from Starbucks and we'd be off until naptime, when we'd pack back into the car and I'd drive and listen to music long after we could be home, the kids clutching newly turned red leaves or an apple from the orchard in their hands as they fell into a slumber, just to enjoy the alone time, the quiet.

Somewhere along the lines, we stopped adventuring as much. We went down to one car when Lucas started working part-time from home, even before the pandemic. On the days he'd work from home, none of us wanted to go far, we liked having him around. And then we became beholden to our schedules. Karate lessons, homeschool co-ops, playdates with friends, music lessons, the to-do list to meet requirements for the kids' education. It was all necessary, all wonderful, but we lost some of the freedom that made homeschooling appealing in the first place.

During the first week Ted was in the hospital, there was one day that Lucas and I were both home and instead of working, he took the day to just be with us. Fynn had plans with friends, so we dropped him off, and then the three of us, Lucas, Paige, and I, filled our afternoon with window shopping and walking around various places. It was a sun-drenched day, and by the time the four of us were back together in the car for the ride home, we were all exhausted. At one point I looked behind me to the backseat and saw both kids were fast asleep, just like all those years ago. The visuals, the backdrop of a week at the hospital, going into a weekend and then another week of unknowns, the emotion of it all overwhelmed me.

Today is one of those glorious September days in Maine that we wait for all year. In the morning the air is finally crisp, but as the day goes on the sunshine warms you through and we strip layers and smile at every corner of the earth.

I'm feeling fragile though, my skin feels thin, and I'm not alone. The beauty of the day is almost too much, and tears escape a few times. Paige and I hold hands more than we normally do. We talk about her Papa, and how he would have loved a day like today. He loved being near the water.

When we arrive on the island we take the only available parking space, like it was being saved just for us. We throw food into our bags and start walking. We make a few stops, one for lunch, but then we continue on a path that takes you around the island. We pass benches with memorial plaques, a wooded area that has been filled with tiny fairy houses made of sticks and other brush, and walk carefully around landslides cascading down cliffs to the water's edge that have been marked with yellow caution tape for walkers to avoid. I follow Paige, whose long legs move much faster than mine. I'm also simply moving slowly, my body is feeling the weight of the last few months, as well as the backpack I've filled with books,

233

my laptop, and lunch. Paige slows down and gives me
a smirk while I catch up to her. I roll my eyes, but she
stays with me as we walk on, eventually making it to a bit
of a pier that juts out from the island. There's a wooden
stairwell down to a rocky beach, with a feather poking out
of the railing. The sky meets the sea in nearly a perfect
match of color. We walk out and sit at the end of the pier,
dangling our legs over the edge, and watch what looks to
be a loon preen itself, and then swim away in search of
fish. On our walk back to the car we decide Ted would have
spent the afternoon sitting out on his porch with his aviator
sunglasses, pipe in hand, quietly staring out at the coast. It
was the kind of day he loved, blue skies that matched his
eyes, a gentle breeze, and an unhurried afternoon.

On the first day of autumn, we pull out the few
fall decorations we have and switch the current placemats
for ones that boast a red pickup truck with pumpkins in
the back. There's an apple-shaped gourd that now sits on
our coffee table and a spoon rest shaped like a maple leaf.
I almost forgot about the equinox, and kick myself for
not celebrating it in a more memorable way. No one else

mentions it, the lack of celebration, and I don't dwell on it for long.

Mary Lou comes over for lunch, and she brings with her a trunk full of items to look through, including some of Ted's coats. He loved his jackets. Lucas also loves jackets and coats; his tee shirts might be threadbare, his jeans worn through, but his jackets… his jackets are always well-fitting, stylish, and matched to any occasion. Out of the pile, Fynn picks out a black wool coat, and Paige grabs a raincoat that has an "I love the national parks" patch on the front. Mary Lou brought other items full of meaning, like two jars of pear jelly that Ted canned years ago, made from the fruit of their pear tree in New Hampshire, and some of Ted's rings. They're hefty, all of the things, filled with memories and love and personality.

It's the first time Mary Lou has been to our house by herself, and when she leaves a few hours later Lucas and I look at each other with eyes full of tears. "I hate that she's going home alone," I say.

Lucas puts his arms around me and whispers, "I know."

Later in the week, I come across a quote by Shannon Beaty that stops me in my tracks, "And when I turned to face grief, I saw that it was just love in a heavy coat."

The next time I walk by the wool coat that now hangs on our coat rack I catch a familiar whiff of pipe smoke and maybe aftershave. Love in a heavy coat, indeed.

On Sunday morning we end up taking our time as we walk, there are no meetings for Lucas to get back to, no errands for me to run, and we stroll down through Lower Field and onto the Bucket Trail. It's been a while since we've walked by the river, it's lower and slower than it's been all year. The path is littered with thin branches, and a few early leaves dot the ground. Back here in the woods, while you can catch a trace of traffic in the breeze if you get quiet, it's peaceful. The countless metal buckets hanging from trees along the path speak to how nature can take over a space when left alone. I can hear the birds sing above, and mushrooms of a dozen varieties are sprinkled throughout. There are shocks of purple spray paint on some of the trees facing the river, there to let anyone who wanders by know that this is private property. In the winter months when the river freezes over we hear snowmobiles racing up and down the makeshift highway. Many years ago there may have been more people using this trail, but now, it's just us. My hope is our footsteps land lighter than those before us, and that we can work with the natural world to coexist in this space. I don't mind its overgrowth if it doesn't mind my gentle steps and Darcey's leaps.

Looking down when I walk so as not to trip on the downed branches, I notice my boots don't even leave an imprint. The forest floor is covered in pine needles that act as a layer of protection, maybe going both ways, softening my footfalls for the earth as well as my knees.

We double back on the trail to make our way back through the fields and up Sledding Hill towards the house. Walking through Lower Field I wonder to myself when the next cutting will be, as the first frost looms. It'll be soon, I tell myself.

That afternoon I'm sitting in the bedroom reading. There's a football game on the television, and Paige is making pumpkin bread, the whir of the hand mixer in the kitchen drowns out the other noises that have become background noise to our Sundays. The neighbors across the way have kept up with their hobby, and we're all getting more used to the occasional gunshots, even Darcey. That is, until we're not. When they get close enough to interrupt phone calls and concentration, when they're loud enough to hear over the hand mixer and the football game, that's when Darcey starts racing around the house looking for a safe space. She ends up in the basement where she climbs onto a shelf lined with empty mason jars. Her eyes are wild, and it takes two of us to get her down safely, but not a single jar falls or breaks. Somehow she stepped so carefully over and between the jars, even though she was filled with such fright.

Darcey and I find solace in the bathroom with the door shut, fans on, and classical music blasting from my phone. All I can think about is the way the pine needles cushioned my step, the birds sang through the trees, and the water sparkled as it flowed downriver earlier.

Monday morning, our daily walk supports us as we start the week. Darcey carefully makes her way out the garage door. "It's safe," we tell her, as we cast a watchful eye across the street.

At the top of Hobbit Hill Lucas stops and points, "It's been cut," he says. It takes me a minute to realize what he's talking about, but when I do I smile. Just yesterday, that sense of knowing swept over me, and it feels like I'm understanding the cycle of things, the way things work on our land.

Later that day the kids, my mother, and I go apple picking over at Ricker Hill Orchard, where we spent the first day of August blueberry picking. We drive past the blueberry bushes to the top of the hill where we can park and see the full extent of the mountain views on offer. The trees are heavy with fruit, some ripened, some still not quite. There are countless varieties, some look like wooden apples you'd put out for decoration, and the array of colors makes for a seasonal rainbow of shades of reds. The kids disappear in the rows, and it's just me and Mom for a while. I hold her bag as she picks. The sound of crunching through the skin and into the flesh of the apple tells me she's taken a break from picking. I turn and she's gazing out at the view.

"Your father needs to see this," she tells me, her eyes wide. It's her first time up the hill. I said the same thing after the kids and I found this place just a few weeks after we moved. It's the kind of view you'd never know existed just five minutes from our house. Sometimes when you're so busy living you forget to take a drive up a mountain to see things from a different perspective.

Mom then tells me how good the apple is, but then she winces, "Sorry," she says. She knows I can't eat them, thanks to an Oral Allergy Syndrome that popped up for me as a young adult.

"It's okay," I say, smiling. I haven't tasted apples in years, but I have such fond memories of apple picking as a child, the endless apple bakes my mother used to make, just holding them in my hands is enough to bring me joy. The rest of my house will enjoy the taste of apple crisps and pies and sauce for the next few weeks, and I'll still get to savor the way the house smells even more like home when apples combine with cinnamon and sugar.

It doesn't take long for everyone to fill their bags, and before it's even been an hour we're driving back down the hill towards home. We make note of the leaves, and how they're on the verge of explosion. Colors bleed out now and then, but in a week they'll no longer be contained.

Our second Adventure Day, and the last one of the month, finds me and Paige on the coast once again. This time, at what's ending up being our once-a-season beach, Popham. There's only a handful of cars in the parking lot, but I run across one woman in the restroom who's dressed in a long flowing fluorescent purple dress. She notices the swimsuit I have in my hand and goes on to tell me how the water's nice.

"I only went up to my knees, but it did the trick," she tells me.

I nod and say, "Sometimes that's all you need."

But I know today I need more than knee-deep water.

On the beach, we spread a quilt that lives in the back of the car that we've used as a beach blanket for years. It's made of material my paternal grandmother picked out, and after her death my mom made for my grandfather. When he passed, it was handed down to me and my family. At first, I felt funny using it on the beach, but my mother has always said her quilts are to be used, and I can't help but agree. It washes well and is a dream to curl up in when the sun goes behind the clouds.

Today the clouds are thin, but so is the warmth from the sun. There's a steady breeze that keeps the few bugs that are left at this time of year away.

It's low tide and there's an expanse of sand between us and the water. We watch the sand, water, and seagulls while eating soup out of travel mugs, wrapped up in towels and sweaters.

241

After the sun and soup have warmed me through I strip down to my swimsuit and brave the water. Between us and the sandbar a ways out, the current runs quickly, and while it's mostly shallow there are sections where the water has worn the sand down and created little bathtub-sized indents where the water goes up to my thighs. The water runs so quickly it makes me think twice about submerging, especially as I'm alone since Paige went up for the restroom. So I wait for her, my feet planted in the sand, water making rushing noises as its flow is forced to go around my legs. When Paige returns she stands in the shallows not even a foot from me, her ankles barely covered, while I'm in the thigh-deep indent. It doesn't take me long, first I kneel in the water, and then I lower all the way, tipping back to let my hair and face dunk in, timing it with a deep and even exhale. I come up and instantly feel my mood shift. The water took not only my breath but so many worries away with it.

Back up at the blanket I wrap a towel around my waist and grab the sun-warmed sweater that came off the needles earlier this month. I sigh contentedly, and loudly, as I pull it over my head, and stick my arms through. The taste of the sea is still on my lips, I'm covered in yarn stitched together by my hands, and truly there's nowhere else I'd rather be.

When it's time to leave I'm still wearing the sweater. I throw on the backpack I bought for my trip, and sling our bag of towels over my arm, as we make our way barefoot back to the car it dawns on me how I feel, and I realize in part it's the way I feel in the sweater, the way I know my hair curls from salt water, with my daughter who knows me better than almost anyone else does, heading home from a day well spent. The care I took to choose items for a trip that was not meant to be didn't mean that those things would languish in the closet. In getting clear about what I needed, a practice I've been honing all year, I was honoring myself on a deeper level, and I feel that care and tenderness now, as I have throughout the month in ways I'm sure I'll only be able to decipher as time moves forward.

While this month has not rolled out the way any of us thought it would, it happened the way it needed to. September, with skies as blue as his eyes, will forever be linked with Ted. The core memories made will linger with us for the rest of our days, but will also intertwine with memories from over years past and to come. It has not been the easiest month, by a long shot, but we've grown. We've softened and changed through the month, and we've been reminded of how strong we are because of that softness, what compassion brings to the table in times of turmoil and thereafter.

Turning the calendar to October feels like a bittersweet relief.

October

October starts with a forecast full of sunshine and warm temperatures. The first falls on a Sunday, and while Lucas and Dad are off on some kind of adventure on the property that requires a chainsaw, I decide to tackle the gardens around our house. There's weeding to be done, forsythia to cut back, and hostas to deadhead.

The gardens around the house went the whole summer without attention. After the rhododendrons were established, I didn't do much except for trimming a few iris heads after they bloomed. The previous year I kept up with the weeding and was on top of the hostas blooms. Not this year.

When I think of where all my garden ambitions went, I have to think back as far as May, and my concussion. Between the rain, missing most of May to recover, and then getting swept up into the swing of summer, I never quite found my footing in the garden. I've watched from the sidelines as Mom expanded her vegetable garden, helping here and there, and reaping the benefits.

Now, I'm sitting at the kitchen counter eating my granola and oat milk, when over the speakers comes a deep male voice with a country twang singing words I'm too startled to comprehend. It takes just a few seconds before I realize what happened, and then in another second, the music has stopped. Lucas is out of the house, the kids aren't awake. But I'm laughing to myself as I grab my phone to text Mom.

"Thanks for that bit of country music," I type.

She responds quickly, "I couldn't find that off button fast enough!"

Due to the Bluetooth and internet settings, we all have access to the speakers in both houses and occasionally things like this happen. Sometimes a video from one house gets cast onto a television screen in another house. It always causes the same reaction, a quick startle and then some laughter.

This morning, on the start of our third October here on the property, I'm still laughing about country music, and am thinking about the ways we're connected here. By location, but also how I know what's happening next door. Because of the speaker incident I know what Mom's listening to as she's getting ready for an early dinner with all of us later that day. The music is the kind that's good for spending a few hours in the kitchen, and I know she's slicing up green tomatoes to make a crisp, mixing the crumble, and slow-cooking a beef stew that'll fill our stomachs and souls after a day spent outside. The interconnectedness that we've figured out along the way hasn't been all rainbows and unicorns, but it's something that I don't take for granted. It gets two thumbs up from me and I can imagine hearing Dad saying it's another win for the homestead.

After taking Darcey for a walk where we meet up with Dad and Lucas for a bit, I make my way over to the barn and grab a wheelbarrow and a half dozen garden tools. There's an open-door policy in the barn. While it's technically Mom and Dad's, we've been told that we can use whatever we need. This is our first house, but it's not their first rodeo, not by a long shot. They've accumulated many tools over the years, in addition to what the previous owner left us as well, and because of that Lucas and I haven't had to buy nearly as many things for the upkeep of the house and yard as we would have otherwise. Don't get me wrong, we came to this house with toolboxes and plastic bins full of our tricks and tools, but we never had a garden. We never had a yard we were in charge of maintaining. We never had a place truly of our own, and the things one needs for the uptake of such a space.

While we came with shovels, my parents came with snowblowers.

I get started in one corner, and decide to make my way around the house, and tend to the three gardens along the way. I start pulling weeds, deadhead the hostas, and trim back irises and daylilies. While some may say it's all overgrown, I think it looks like the beginning of autumn in a cottage garden. The expired flowers may look unkempt, but I appreciate how they show the transition of seasons.

As I look back at the spaces I've worked on, it looks neat, but something is missing, some character and nuance. Maybe it's because we're coming towards the end of a year that hasn't gone as planned, that's thrown us some blows. I probably look a little unkempt most days, as does the inside of the house. There are dust bunnies and dog hairs in the corners of every room. The house isn't as spotless as it was for the first year we lived here. Life has kept going, and instead of saying I haven't been able to keep up, I'm trying to look at it as a lived-in house, a lived-in life.

Paige joins me, gardening gloves in hand. We work side by side, sometimes talking, but mostly quietly. She's following my lead and asks plenty of questions.

"If you accidentally cut something you don't think you should have - it's okay," I tell her, "it'll grow back next year. Remember, it doesn't have to be perfect," I say.

We talk about the plans for the coming week, including the start of her driver's ed course, what Grammy is making for dinner, and the latest drama with her friends. Big and small things get mixed into these working moments, these lived moments.

The next few hours go by in a blink. Paige calls it a day, and I'm by myself for a few when I start to feel my body talking. I push through, and at the end, there are enough weeds and sticks and flower bits to fill the back of the buggy, let alone a wheelbarrow. Just as I'm finishing for the day, Lucas and Dad are finishing as well. They're covered in dirt and grime, but their smiles are wide and their stories are as colorful as any of our flower gardens.

Lucas and I drive the buggy, its back end filled with garden debris, down to the brush pile at the edges of

Lower Field. Afterward, he drives us around the fields, something we haven't done in months. There is nothing like walking the fields, taking them step by step, and grounding yourself in them. But there's also nothing like being driven around in a buggy with just a roll cage over you, the wind whipping through your hair and at your cheeks. I look over at Lucas, and he's got a subtle smile on his face that's etched with dirt and fatigue.

I know we're both the kind of tired we haven't been for a while - physically more than emotionally.

Last month when we said the trees would explode in color, we were right. Not yet at peak, the colors are a balm for the soul. Reds and oranges, greens and yellows, they're subtle and sweet until the light hits just so and the colors turn vibrant.

There's a combination of movement and solitude that's calling to me. Our October calendar is full of appointments and things that I couldn't handle last month that got shoved into the deal with later pile. It's later now, and the pile of things needing my attention grows every day, just like the swaths of color expand across tree-lined roads.

It's the middle of the week and it's a beautiful day. The sun is shining, and I have nowhere to be for a bit of time, so I put my boots on and head out the door. It's humid, and the mosquitoes are back, but neither of those things stops me. I don't even offer to take the dog with me. Maybe it's that I'm reading *Windswept: Walking the Paths of Trailblazing Women* by Annabel Abbs, but I want to walk, to feel my feet fall on the ground, to find quiet, and to get lost in familiar territory. The book is on loan from Gina, and the author weaves her story in with the tales of nine women - authors and artists - who took to the outdoors for a myriad of reasons. Their stories, particularly regarding their walking adventures, are little known, and the author explores the reasons why, as well as the challenges they faced due to their sex. Between navigating menstrual cycles on the trail, to the dangers that women navigate simply by being a woman, to the attitudes and shaming that occur when women break societal expectations, it has always been no small feat for a woman to break out on their own, particularly in the wilderness.

251

Walking on our trails with the stories I've been reading in mind, I'm grateful for the peace of mind granted by our boundary lines. I can almost guarantee I won't see another person on my walk, and there's a good possibility that crunching through the leaves will scare off any wildlife that might be brave enough to say hello. Even still, I have a collapsed baton at easy reach just in case.

After walking down from Hobbit Hill, I find myself in Upper Field. I turn to the right and go up towards the property line that abuts a fenced-in area our neighbors use for their horses. A little way before the fence, I nearly trip over a wayward apple. It's bigger than a crab apple, and my eyes search the trees just in case, even though it doesn't seem likely there's an apple tree. Low and behold, stuffed in and among the aspens, birch, maple, and handful of pine trees is what looks like a single branch of an apple tree with two apples hanging off its branches. I reach further in the trees, but it's too much of a jumble of limbs and darkness to see where the trunk lies. I look over my shoulder to see if anyone else is seeing what I'm seeing, and then roll each of the apples off the stem. They both fit in my hands, and I carry my treasure with me as I continue. Rounding the corners of the fields, I find myself thinking I need to take the apples to my parent's house to show them the fruits of the stray apple tree.

For as long as I can remember I've craved quiet, and yet at the same time when I come out of the time alone, I feel just as much of a craving to share my experience, to connect with others. It's a push and pull that doesn't always feel logical, and at the same time, as soon as I gather with others, I'm almost always looking forward to the time I can be alone again. And yet, there are times when I'm bursting with stories to share, and I can't wait to tell someone. I remember countless times I've shared just a story, and it's not met with the enthusiasm I held for it, and have felt the heat of shame and remorse flood through my body. Not that there was any shame in telling the story, but it's maybe about the second-guessing one does when sharing something that meant something to them with someone who doesn't appreciate the same things or is open to someone's enthusiasm.

Years ago Mary Lou and Ted took us on a lighthouse tour on the coast of Maine. I said something about always having wanted to live on an island with a lighthouse, and the guide overheard and made a comment to the effect of not many people are made of the kind of stuff to do that, it's not as romantic as everyone thinks. My mother-in-law raised an eyebrow and said, "If anyone could handle it, she could." The two of us shared a look and some laughter.

By the time I finish my rounds of the fields, I can feel sweat dripping down my back. My lungs are full of humid air and my heart rate is up as I make my way to my parent's house. I knock on the door and let myself in, peering into their house from the mudroom so the dirt from my boots doesn't dirty their floors.

But no one's home. The house is quiet. I think about leaving the apples on the counter, maybe writing a note. But then there's another part of me that's not ready to hand them over. Instead, I take the apples home and set them on our kitchen counter. I poke my head into the office to find the telltale signs of a meeting in progress, the cord of Lucas's earphones frames his face. One of the kids is out at an activity, the other is taking a nap. I sigh with impatience, but with my next breath, my shoulders pull down from my ears. Maybe it's not a bad thing to keep my findings to myself for just a bit longer. They'll hear about it in due time. My heart flutters and swells with the idea that the fruits of the field are just for me for a few moments longer.

The humidity bleeds into a rainy weekend. It's a celebratory weekend - the first of three birthdays that come one after another is mine. Lucas and the kids ask me what I want to do, but honestly, I don't feel like celebrating. Nonetheless, I'm feeling the anticipation I've always felt leading up to my birthday, which makes for conflicting feelings all around. Lucas has always done his best to spoil me on Mother's Day and my birthday, but I know how tired he is. I know he's still catching up from the last two months, body-wise, heart-wise, and soul-wise. At the same time, I'm so tired of making decisions, of planning dinners and days and activities, I wish for a fairy godmother to come in and whip my unspoken and unknown dreams into reality.

Instead, I ask for a quiet day spent reading and knitting, lunch and cake with my parents, leftovers for dinner. Paige, our resident baker, makes a pumpkin cake with caramel icing, and it's divine. The kids give me books and yarn, their choices make me smile. Lucas makes me breakfast after which we take Darcey for a walk, and he checks in multiple times to see if I need anything. I'm grateful for his presence and attentiveness, but my heart is still heavy, knowing his is, too.

The day passes like many quiet Sundays we've

spent in this house. The rain blows over and we have lunch outside on my parent's deck. I'm gifted a card from my parents with a photo of me several lifetimes ago. It's me when I was thirteen or fourteen, up in an apple tree. We pick our dates for the next round of the Liquid Crystalline Prognosticator Extrordinaire award, choosing when each of us think we'll get our first six inches of snow. Sitting outside in the autumn air, it's hard to imagine snow and the change of seasons is just around the corner.

Later I'm sitting on a couch with a book at one end of the house, there's football coming from the other and without seeing I know Lucas is stretched out, his eyes are probably drooping. The kids are upstairs, taking time to themselves after a family meal. We're together at home, but separate. There's peace in that, but I also feel swells of guilt about not orchestrating a weekend of activities for everyone. There were no pumpkin patch visits, no family walks through the woods listening to leaves crunching beneath our feet. Such is life in a family of introverts. So often we are together, but separate. Within shouting distance, but just out of reach.

But I know that eventually a kid will come downstairs and plop down on the other end of the couch from me. I know that Lucas will stretch his legs and walk over my way just to plant a kiss on my lips. I know Darcey will mosey in, looking for love by way of belly rubs. I know the need for snacks will bring another kid downstairs, and they'll check in to see how my afternoon is going. It's what we do.

We go our separate ways, but we always circle back to one another. There's a perpetual turning back towards one another for a check-in. A constant searching for each other's eyes, a gentle touch, a quiet way of being together.

This quiet way of tending to each other, of awareness of each other, and our needs is the basis for having the strength and ability to move through the world gently - because it's a supported way. This family of mine, we know each other's hearts. Moving through the world knowing you're seen and understood, even by just a handful of people, can make a huge difference. When you see yourself reflected by the people who love you, and that image matches or is even better than how you view yourself, that's powerful.

But sometimes, it gets fuzzy. Sometimes life can get in the way, and the reflection coming back at you is hazy and rough around the edges, and it's an opportunity to get quiet, go within, and check in with yourself. Search for your own eyes, and give yourself the loving check-in you offer others.

      Earlier in the month, buoyed by Lucas's comments and the encouragement from my writing partner, Gina, I dove into the third draft of the novel. This time I'm cleaning up language and shoring up plot points, clarifying sections and consistencies. It's concrete work, and it's something I can wrap my head around. In the notebook I keep specifically for this novel, I list out all the chapters with open squares next to each one that I can throw a sticker on upon completion. There's an objective, and though it's not based on word count like a first draft might be, there's a goal and something attainable I can check off the list each time I sit down to work. A chapter a session isn't a problem. Going through grammar and phrasing, while mind-bending at times, is a different type of work than the creation of the first draft, the creation of a world and characters, and moving a story forward. There is a set of rules to follow in some ways, it's straightforward during a time when I need the comfort of known entities.

We're not sleeping well. In particular, I'm not sleeping well. There are outward reasons for the first few nights: the dog, a snoring partner thanks to the change in the seasons and his lingering cold, a squirrel that's found its way into the wall behind our headboard. But then one night I find myself still awake at three in the morning. I've tried all my tricks, I've come out to the couch to sleep alone, as it sometimes helps, I've read and read and read and my eyelids still haven't dropped an inch. It's not caffeine consumption or lack of exercise. It's my brain. It's so full - it feels like I need to hit a release valve to let the steam out, but I don't know where the valve is located.

Within a week and a few gusty winds, we've passed peak leaf foliage. The brilliant colors lasted just long enough to catch them in the right light, and then they faded to a more subdued, vintage palette. Driving around, we're closer to stick season than not, and it feels appropriate that it's coming upon us quickly this year. If I blinked at just the right moment, I might have missed the gorgeous colors on the tree lines last week. If I hadn't been out for a drive on a sunny day… if I hadn't had my eyes open.

How often do we have our eyes open?

Our hearts?

Our minds?

Without the buffer of rest, with the way the layers of grief we're going through as a family unfold and peel away… there are choices in every moment of whether or not to feel the feelings or to blink them away.

On one of our Adventure Days, Paige and I end up with half an hour free, and so we find a local trail to stretch our legs on instead of sitting in a parking lot. We head out on the path towards Hedgehog Mountain, but we know we won't make it far. Fifteen minutes in and back, we tell ourselves. We go slowly, and it feels like one of those walks we took years ago, a noticing walk where the kids would name everything they saw, everything they noticed. Today we point out mushrooms, the way exposed roots form crevasses that hold fallen leaves, and a dog with three legs who runs at full speed alongside his able-bodied dog friend. Paige falls over herself with laughter while she tells me a story about a friend of hers, teenage - but really, human - antics. We're all just human, at different stages of becoming.

It's overcast, as is what's feeling like every October afternoon, and as it gets to be time to turn around we notice a tunnel of aspen aglow in the gloom in front of us. We both stop and take in the colors, I try to take a photo but the camera doesn't do the colors justice, doesn't do the moment justice.

October feels like it's too hard to accurately portray in a photograph, or even in descriptive words.

By the time we make it back to the car, the fresh air has worked out any kinks from the day. That thirty minutes with Paige in the woods was by far the best part of the day.

Later that week, Jess and I meet up at the Androscoggin Riverlands State Park with backpacks full of lunches and knitting. I haven't seen her since our overnight exploring yarn shops just before the phone call that changed everything, and we have much to catch up on. We both have hiking boots and flannel shirts on, and we both look like we belong right where we are.

The main trail is frequented by ATVs, so we find a smaller path, the Homestead Trail, that takes us along the river and into the woods where there was once a home where now all that's left is the foundation. It's a Saturday morning, but there's hardly anyone else on the smaller trail, a few couples and dog walkers, but mostly we're alone with our conversation and the trees.

Jess and I find ourselves in front of a pond, and we joke about some cold wild swimming. Maybe another day, we say. We end up at the homestead site where we sit on the foundation stones and get out our knitting. She's working on a scarf, I'm working on socks, and neither of us has to look at our hands or stitches while we talk. We talk about knitting, life, kids, husbands, family, friends, our hopes and dreams, and the obstacles we face and want to overcome. We don't shy away from the heaviness of life, of our midlife realities, but we also don't hide from the lighter corners.

For us though, it always comes back to knitting. Neither of us has a wide circle of fiber friends, and so it's always heartening to be able to speak the same language. We can poke a little fun at one another for our proclivities: the colors we're always drawn to, the projects we avoid, and how we do or do not swatch before starting a project.

Since about mid-September, when I finished the sweater, the only things that have been on my needles have been socks. The ones I'm working on now are my fourth pair, all the same pattern. It's a simple ribbed sock with a Fleegle heel, it's designed by one of my favorite Maine designers and the fit is the best I've ever had in a hand-knit sock. While I haven't memorized the numbers within the pattern, I know the movements by heart. In these last few weeks, I haven't been able to look at anything more complicated. I needed known projects, easy books to read, straightforward recipes for our meals, simple directions, and clear ways forward. Editing the third draft of my novel provides structure and consistency to my work days, and the knitting fills in the gaps of the long evenings, the hours between dinner, and when it's acceptable to turn out the lights.

I need the sock knitting as much as I don't need a complicated pattern.

Jess doesn't knit socks. She's attempted a few, and we've laughed about her results.

"Would you want a pair of socks?" I ask her as the sun streams through the trees, my fingers pause between stitches. "I know you don't enjoy knitting them, but I thought maybe I could knit you a pair."

Her face brightens, "I was wondering if you'd want to do a sort of swap," she says. I nod my head, smiling over the fact that we're on the same page. "It's just," she continues, "that we're always knitting, but how often do people knit for us?"

I agree. Knitters have preferences, and we're a bit quirky. We also don't want to waste our time knitting something for someone who won't appreciate the object, or simply won't wear it for whatever reason. While knitters appreciate other knitter's work, we tend to like what we like, know others like what they like, and knit for ourselves because it's easier.

We sit in the woods and work out the details of a swap. We're both excited, and I can't wait to start knitting a pair of socks for Jess out of a skein of yarn I picked up while we were on our adventure at the end of August. I want to knit gratitude and memories and wishes for so many things into these socks so she can feel the love they hold when she wears them.

That's what gift knitting is about.

That's what friendship is about.

Knitting friendship into objects is just about the most fulfilling thing a knitter can do.

The next day I bring Lucas, the kids, and Darcey back to the state park. The trail was so pretty and so close to home, that I want them to experience something different than our usual walk around our property. Darcey doesn't get out much, and the car ride alone is a big thing for her. But we get on the trail and she sniffs to her heart's content and her confidence grows with every step. We got out of the house relatively early, but neither of the kids complains. Paige wears Ted's old raincoat and her red Converse sneakers that blend in with the fallen foliage, Fynn wears aviator sunglasses and a corduroy jacket. Everyone's quiet, except for cheering on Darcey, telling her what a good job she's doing navigating the new trail. Maybe we're cheering on each other, not just her.

We stay for an hour, make it just past the homestead foundation and back, long enough for Darcey to feel like it's familiar enough to bark at a young couple who pass on on the trail.

It feels like a win, getting out on a Sunday morning. It feels like a win to move our bodies, to feel fresh, crisp air in our lungs, to take in sights and sounds that are different from the ones in our backyard. We get so entrenched in our routines, in what's right in front of us, that we forget that there's a world outside of our own.

Lucas's birthday comes next. That morning we give Lucas gifts before he starts his workday: a hat with an LED light in the brim and a pair of socks from Renys - "A Maine Adventure" boasts their ads - a book of poems by Mary Oliver, and a print of a tiger wearing a flower crown that made the kids and me think of him.

It's midweek, and while Fynn and I are out of the house all day, Paige opts to stay home and bake a black forest cake from scratch. When we come back home we find Lucas grilling, and Paige is inside working on other components of dinner. There's a cake on the counter, music playing through Bluetooth speakers, it feels like a celebratory day even though we spent it like any other midweek day of the week.

We sit and share a meal, we sing Happy Birthday to Lucas, and we laugh over the candles Paige picked out. Normally, we use big chunky number candles that show the birthday person's age. This time we didn't have the exact numbers, so she placed a four and then two other numbers that would add up to the number eight. But without parentheses, it looks like Lucas is turning four hundred seventy-one. We laugh, all four of us, until the dog comes out from her resting spot under the table to check on us.

Little moments full of big joy, we take them when we can.

The colors are hanging on, still surprising us during a week when we're away from the house more often than not, up and down 95, through familiar back roads, appointments, and activities. Life is full, but the kind of full that feels like you can't wrap your head around it before it expands even more. A season of expansion before the contraction of winter, where the elements keep us inside more than out.

We're in a pattern of cloudy days, but even when the sun shines, its strength has diminished, though it still has the power to make those lingering leaves glow so vividly it takes your breath away.

After weeks of playing catch-up in all departments, it feels like I've been able to grab hold of some semblance of routine. It's counter-intuitive, but I find it easier to wake up in the wee hours of the morning when it's dark, and so I've been starting the day before the sun comes up when the house and the world are seemingly at peace. There's something about chilly, dark mornings, illuminated by twinkle lights or candles, that entices me. Summer mornings have a different quality to them, they tend to invite slow starts after late nights, no matter how early the sun rises. Maybe it's that I can't get ahead of the game on those mornings when the sun rises so early. Lately, it feels like if I watch the sun slowly spread across the sky I'm moving with the day, not trying to catch up to it, if that makes sense. If I watch the transition from darkness to light, and then back again, if I witness the unfolding of the day, I'm more likely to witness the unfolding of myself as well.

We comment to each other that we can't remember there being as many rust-colored pine needles on the ground in years passed. This year, they're everywhere, a cushioned path for us to walk on. They also serve as decoration. Many of the pine trees have empty lower branches, and as the dried pine needles make their way down, they get stuck on the bare branches, giving them adornment once more. The clumps of pine needles end up looking like V's straddling the branches, nature's tinsel.

The leaves are like so many things, not this or that. While they're not in peak season, they're not completely off the branches, and they're still beautiful. Some are completely at their peak and haven't gone along with the crowd. There's wind and rain in the forecast for the upcoming weekend, and we know that means most of the colors - no matter what stage they're in - will be gone come Monday.

Lit candles and strings of twinkle lights illuminate a dreary Sunday, though it's bright outside the windows thanks to the leaves that are still turning colors. I offer walks, but no one takes me up on the offer, canine or human. Instead of going out in the rain by myself, I cuddle up in bed with a heating pad, a hot cup of tea, and my book.

Early in the week, there's frost on the ground, it hangs onto blades of grass and leaves edges well past sunrise. Hunting season is upon us, so we switch up our walking routine and add in a long lead for Darcey. She wears an orange coat, but we still keep her close. We don't know what she'll do if she hears a shot when we're on a

walk, and we're afraid she'll bolt back to the house. Better
to keep her close. We walk with bright colors ourselves,
Lucas in his orange hat, me in a neon pink fleece. We go
slower with Darcey on the leash. She knows not to run and
so we're not trying to catch up to her. We don't need to
catch our breath after climbing up Sledding Hill. Slow and
steady is the season we're in.

It's later in the week, and the weather has taken a
turn. There's no longer frost in the forecast, instead, there's
a three-day period of highs above 60 degrees. Thursday
morning we wake up thinking we're still dreaming. The
night before, a shooter killed eighteen people and wounded
many more just twenty minutes from us at a bowling alley
and a bar. We went to bed with heads full of what-ifs,
locked our doors, and hugged the kids extra tightly. We're
far enough away from the locations directly impacted to
feel safe, even as the search for the shooter goes on, but
close enough that everything in our town - and indeed,
most of the state - has shut down.

After watching a press conference, tears fresh on
my cheeks, I take Darcey outside. We stay close to the

house, and we're both a bit out of sorts. The temperature makes it feel like June and not October. Traffic on the main road is nonexistent. It's eerily quiet. But just as I step outside a half dozen ladybugs land on my arms. I look over at the exterior of the house, and it's covered in ladybugs, they're swarming around. Darcey just stands in the grass, unsure of what to do, looking to me for direction but I have none.

Later in the afternoon Lucas and I take her for a walk. While we know the manhunt is happening more east of us, and that we're safe, there are still possibilities we can't wrap our heads around. Logically I know the suspect is not hiding out on our property, but I wouldn't have taken a walk through our woods and fields alone today.

The past few times we've gone down Chickadee Lane we've noticed Cup Fungi in several places. They look like something you'd see under the ocean, and they feel almost like leather, a mix of a silicone mold and seaweed. Today, they catch my eye, as does the blanket of leaves atop the layers of pine needles that fell earlier in the month. There's a whole world at and under our feet. Somehow even on this day where my head is filled with man-made terror, my attention is drawn to this other world that exists without any help from us, even despite us. Nature is layered and textured, colorful and detailed, quiet and industrious.

The day passes, and we're searching for news and explanations, but at the end of the evening, we know little more than we did in the morning.

The following day there's a little more traffic on the road, but word comes in of cancellations far and wide, businesses remain closed. More press conferences, seemingly less information. We wonder how long this can go on, how long will the families who are mourning loved ones have to wait for answers, for justice? Someone in the press conference says it'll be a lifetime of healing for many.

How many of us, how many of them, were already in the process of healing for a lifetime? How much more grief, tragedy, and terror can we as a species bear witness to and hold without going numb?

On Friday night, we have a family dinner with my parents. Our plans for dinner need to be changed, as we never made it out to pick up groceries before the stores shut down. We cobble together a meal between our two houses, grilled chicken and a side made up of canned vegetables from Mom's pantry.

We're all different levels of solitary people, and we've gone about the last few days the best we can. Dad's been out in his workshop working on his lathe, Mom's been organizing her house and baking dessert for tonight, the kids have been doing school work and also talking with their friends, and Lucas has been in the office. I've been doing laundry, vacuuming the floors, checking the news, taking Darcey out, writing some words, and knitting. And so when we come together, we allow ourselves a break from simply getting on with things, from surviving. We come together, and we're honoring those who cannot, those who haven't.

By the time Mom and Dad go home later in the evening, it's evident just how much we needed to be together. There's some teary eyes, big hugs, and yes, there's even laughter. We speak questions out loud we've been thinking silently. We come together in our form of community.

Though Dad didn't say it aloud, or gesture with a thumbs up, I couldn't help but think it's another win for the homestead as I watched my parents walk home.

Later that night, long after Mom and Dad have gone home, around 48 hours after the initial horrific event, the shooter is found. He isn't alive. There's a feeling of relief mixed with grief, for the victims, and for our community.

In some ways there's closure, but in so many other ways it feels like this is just the beginning.

As the month comes to a close, I'm wrestling with so many things. I'm trying to stay above water when it comes to my mental health, as well as keeping tabs on the rest of the family's emotions, at least what I can piece together from moods and actions and whatever they share with me. I know I'm not responsible for them all, but I feel strongly about being aware. There's a difference between taking responsibility for other people's stuff, and simply being aware, acknowledging, and supporting. Sometimes I think we get the two confused, especially as caretakers, parents, and partners.

October is my favorite month of the year, but this year I'm ready to put it behind us. It's been busy, and heavy. World events, local events, and the weight of the last few months are all weighing heavily on us.

I'm desperate for relief to come in one form or another, and while I thought October was going to hold that for us, maybe it was too soon to expect such things. As with everything, it's a process, life and grief. When there's an event that brings those emotions to the surface, and then other events one after the other, so much that was bubbling just beneath comes up as well. It feels as though October ushered in all of those things, the things that bubbled beneath that we're too tired to shove back down, but too depleted to process.

Looking back at the month, it was productive. If one were to go by that alone, it could easily be looked at as a success. I've gotten halfway through the third draft of the novel, the book you're reading at this moment has continued to move along steadily, I knit about four pairs of socks, we got back into the routine of school and life, countless appointments were attended, and the list could go on and on.

But beneath the surface, we're still bewildered and weary. It's a true fake it until you make it phase for us all, and I'm not alone in wanting our hearts and minds to catch up to the daily movements of our bodies.

There are moments when I can tell I'm getting there. Last week on the way home from a day out I drove past an older man who was stocking a Free Little Library just outside of what I assume was his house. There was a red light up ahead, so I was slowing down to a stop and had just enough time to see the look of concentration on his face and the care going into the action. It was not a moment where he threw whatever he could inside the little library, there was attention, there was reverence. In the span of a moment or two, I saw the humanity in his movements, in his actions, and it brought me to tears.

I see it in the way the leaves are still hanging on, well after we thought they'd fall off through wind and rain, and how some are still turning from green to golden even in the final days of the month. I see it in the way the empty page embraces whatever thoughts and missives I share. I see it in the way people show up for each other by checking in with texts and phone calls. I see it in the signs downtown that show an outline of the state of Maine with a heart over the towns affected by the recent tragedy. And I see it in the care we take during everyday moments like taking out the dog, brushing our teeth, washing the dishes, folding the laundry, and hugging our children before bed.

These are the moments that touch the spirit, and the more tenderness feel, the closer we are to healing.

November

November starts on a quiet note. A head cold is floating through the house, though Paige and Lucas seem to be spared. Fynn and I, on the other hand, are down for the count - but in different ways. Fynn has a full-on cold, he's stuffy and miserable and goes through a box of tissues a day. Mine is there just enough to slow me down. A bit of a sore throat, some head congestion, and sneezes that make my whole upper respiratory system ache, but it never fully develops.

After a busy October, I don't fight slowing down. There's nothing on our calendar for the remainder of the week, so it feels like my weekend starts early and I just go slowly. By the time Saturday gets here, I'm rested, really and truly.

On Saturday while Lucas is cleaning up the yard - taking decorative pumpkins to the compost bin, bringing in

the outdoor furniture for the coming season, and closing up
the outdoor water tap - Darcey and I head out for a walk.
While the ick lingers, I have energy and the temperatures
are just right: cool enough to keep mosquitoes at bay and
for the frost to linger in shady patches, warm enough that
I don't need to wear layers that might weigh me down
enough to bring on a sense of fatigue. It's late morning, and
I intend to take our normal route down through Chickadee
Lane, but once we get there, there's something in me that
just wants to keep walking. We pass the entrance to the
lane, and when Darcey sniffs in the opposite direction I take
that as a sign to follow a whim instead of routine.

We end up taking a long and leisurely walk around
the perimeter of Lower Field. We go slowly, I don't hurry
her along when she stops to sniff every few feet. While
she's busy, I take in the fresh air, the change in the trees
and lack of foliage from even last week, and how I can
see through to the river, and even through the trees across
the way. The shift in the season, now that we're deeply
entrenched in autumn, shifts perspective.

The field hasn't grown much since the last cutting,
but it's all still green. It doesn't look like it matches the
starkness of the trees, the thinness of the foliage, or the
milky sky that is November.

There is nothing out of the ordinary on our walk. Darcey keeps looking back to check that we're going the right way. "This way," I tell her, "keep going."

We're nearing the end of the year, and it feels like I need that direction too, that refocusing. This way, I tell myself, keep going. We're almost there. In my mind, the last two months of the year blur into one, and at this moment, outside with just my canine companion, I want it all to slow down. I want to notice the way there is no breeze, the way the birds warn of our coming, the way the leaves on the ground no longer hold their red and yellow hues and are now varying shades of brown but they crunch to perfection beneath our feet. I want to notice it all.

Back at home full of fresh air and exercise-induced endorphins I grab the vacuum and start cleaning up the house. October left me depleted in many ways, and the house took a hit by the end of the month. There's tidying to be done, clutter to put away, flannel sheets to put on the beds, and a load of laundry to start. I go slowly, noticing the details inside as much as I did outside, taking as much care with my eyes as my hands. We've been here for two years, are the things I stood in awe of when we first moved in still standing out to me?

I don't know if I like my answer to that question.

Lucas comes in and gives me a questioning look, "You're not doing too much?" he asks.

I shake my head, "No, I'm just about done," I tell him.

We're both still for a moment, both catching our breath, and then we embrace in a sweaty hug. I smile into his chest and say, "We've got a really nice home."

It's a simple statement, but he gives me an extra squeeze before letting go.

"It's good to remember that," he says. He's right. So often we get caught up in the things that feel important, the daily minutia, the things we think we need to do and have to live a beautiful life. Discontent breeds in the swell of new and shiny we're privy to every time we open our emails or social media. Even a spacious home with plenty of room, comfort, and warmth can feel lacking when we turn our attention outward.

The rest of the weekend moves slowly, and there's

an intentionality that's brought to my choices, from where I sit to what occupies my hands to make an effort to connect with our home and its inhabitants in a way that tells them and me that I'm choosing them. I'm choosing this place. I'm choosing to be here, with them, and myself. I'm choosing to not look away. I'm choosing to give them, and myself, my presence.

After a year of trying to notice my habits and tendencies deeply, I recognize that it's a gift I don't always give freely.

I don't know what it is about the last few days, maybe the cold has dulled that part of me that looks outward for what I should be doing. But there's a definite change in view and I can't pinpoint its origin.

We turn the clocks back an hour and find ourselves in the long dark evenings of November. Long gone are the days of managing little ones and time changes, but the shift into the darker evening hours calls out for coziness, and there's nothing more cozy than steaming mugs of cocoa and tea gathered around a table with card games, Darcey snoozing at our feet. So Sunday night all four of us play cribbage after dinner. We end the weekend with laughter, lingering sniffles, and the gift of each other's presence. We might not know what exactly the next week will bring, but whatever happens, we'll have had these moments. Nothing can take them away.

Midweek cold weather rolls in on the wind, threatening temperatures below freezing and even snow. None of us believe it'll snow, but stranger things have happened.

It's a blustery day, and Fynn is getting ready to go out on a four-mile hike at the coast. My parents have errands to run in the town where we drop off Fynn for his outdoor education classes, so they offer to take him and save me a trip.

While we're waiting for Dad to pull their car out of the garage, I ask Fynn, "Did you pack layers?"

"Yes," he says.

"Did you have a hat and mittens?"

"Yes."

"Lunch?"

"Yes."

"Are you sure you have a hat?"

He smiles down at me because that's how tall he is.

"I do. You raised me well," he says kindly, not a hint of an eye roll in sight. He knows my questions are all code for I love you.

I don't have a reply. I know we're not done with the raising of him or his sister. But we're getting closer, and that alone makes me wonder what else I can do to make sure these young people have what they need to venture out in the world, and how can I make sure they know they will always have a safe place to return, here with us?

I reach for him, for a hug, and he envelops me with his long arms, his svelte frame, and all those layers of him. They shed a little bit when he hugs me tightly, and I can feel that little boy and his great big expressions of love that bowled me over with such energy and force all those years ago.

"Be safe, have fun," I say into his shoulder.

"I will. Love you, too, Mom," he says.

And I think to myself, he knows.

The next day we get our first snow. It's not

predicted to accumulate too much, but when the snow starts falling from the sky there's a palpable excitement in the atmosphere. The first snow. We're slated to get a whopper of a winter with it being an El Nino year, but even with the long winter ahead the first snowfall is a marker of magic and wonder that I can't ignore.

Paige has her final hours with a driving instructor to earn her learner's permit, but the snow does little to dampen her mood. "It's good practice," we all say. And it is. I drop her off and watch her get into the driver's seat of the Driver's Ed vehicle. The snow falls in wet clumps on the windshield, but it's not the reason for my blurred vision. Regardless, I turn the wipers on, and the snow streaks across the glass as I dab at my eyes.

An hour later I'm sitting in the backseat of the instructor's car. This is the optional observation hour for parents, to see how your teenager is doing before they're given their permit and back to you to oversee seventy hours of driving. Paige has warned me that her instructor doesn't say much. We are both used to filling silences with questions and observations, but by her tone, it seems that's unnecessary and unwanted in this situation. On the drive over Paige asked if I was nervous about this part. "No," I told her, and I was honest. "Your brother has broken me in over the last year and a half," I joke. But it's true. This isn't my first rodeo. So it goes for the second child.

Paige pulls away from the curb and follows the instructor's quiet but clear directions. Easy on the curve. Take this right. Stay in the close lane.

I picked the seat behind her, and so I have a clear view of the instructor instead of Paige. I watch for his subtle movements that show he's human, his hand raises ever so slightly when Paige drives close to the lines on the road, and then he settles as she corrects herself. I know those movements, they're the same ones I use when I'm in the passenger seat, even when Lucas is driving. It's not that I don't trust him, or Fynn and Paige's driving. I don't trust the other drivers, and maybe the roads themselves.

Af I'm honest, it's not that I don't trust anyone else, it's that I don't trust that anyone will see what I'm seeing. Whether it's a red light, a car pulling out in front of us, a sigh at the dinner table, the change in tone during a conversation, the implied, the hint of expectation, the ice on the road...

Instead of watching the instructor for the whole hour, I settle into the seat, look out the window, and choose to trust. There's nothing I can do but trust. It's a feeling I'm having to get more comfortable with as the kids get older, as we all get older and hopefully wiser. The light snow eventually turns to sleet, it pings off the windshield and the roof of the car. My window starts to get blurred with streaks, but the golden hues of November remain thanks to the pumpkins and wayward leaves we pass.

The hour goes by quickly, and without event, we're back at our starting place and Paige is being handed her temporary permit. Later, she'll be initiated into the club of those of us who sit and wait at the Bureau of Motor Vehicles to get her actual permit. But for now, this official piece of paper signifies the end of Driver's Ed and the beginning of her hours with us.

There's a hint of nerves at play in my stomach that brings me back to the early days with each kid at the hospital after their births when we looked at the nurses and then back at our infants thinking, are we allowed to take them home? Are they fully in our care? Are we ready? Are they?

I want to ask the instructor if he thinks she's ready, but I squash the question and trust what I just witnessed with my own eyes. My daughter drove for an hour in all sorts of conditions, speed limits, and traffic patterns with no incident.

"Do you want to drive us home?" I ask.

She hesitates, but it doesn't take long before she's got the keys and is adjusting the driver's seat of our Subaru.

I ask her if she's ready, and watch as her eyes light up the dreary November day.

"I'm ready," she says.

And I know without a doubt, she is, and this next step into a season of unknowns is bittersweet in so many ways. Somehow the weather, the damp cold that finds its way into your bones when you shiver and reach for what is known and comfortable, feels fitting for this moment. With the discomfort that comes with having a new driver there's also the knowledge of their hard work and perseverance, and the remembering and trusting of all the things you've instilled in them and how it's mixed with their knowing and strengths, it all wraps around me like a blanket. I can't tell if it's that or the seat warmers that take the edge off the cold as we make our way home through the farmlands and mountain views that feel more like home with every milestone we cross.

I've always wanted to write, but I haven't always written. For as long as I can remember, writing has been what I wanted to do in life, but between high school and motherhood, I wrote very little other than college essays. When Fynn was a baby I started writing a blog mostly for myself and family members. Quickly it became a creative outlet during a time when losing myself to diapers and breastfeeding was a very real outcome. By the time Paige was born, I was writing regularly on my blog, and starting to think about writing in new ways. I began taking online courses as well as in-person workshops, then came National Novel Writing Month where I proved to myself that I could write lots and lots of words that turned into a novel.

In the meantime, we became a homeschooling family and participated in activities, play dates, field trips, and all the things. I was present for them while also finding pockets of the day to tend to my writing life, to myself. In doing so I showed the kids that our interests matter, our passions matter, and that we could respect each other and what we worked on individually as well as communally, whether it was a novel, Legos, video games, craft projects, or baking cookies.

I have never regretted my writing time, and I have never regretted time spent with my children. Motherhood and writing are inextricably linked for me, and they inform one another. I have learned more about myself from these two endeavors than any other in my life, and am better for all of the days spent finding time for both.

My writing life was born from the early days of motherhood, and as one never stops mothering in some way, one doesn't stop being a writer, either. It's a way of being, a way of seeing, a way of living. Walking through the world, I use words to make sense of it all. And while I'm sure there would have been another catalyst had I not become a mother, I appreciate the link these two vocations have created.

Whether it's through journaling or fiction or stringing words together in my head as I walk through the woods, when the current depth of season swells - in parenting, marriage, friendships, self-exploration - the words guide me home. As I walk our well-worn paths out back, I'm reminded of phrases that jumped out at me, ahha moments that arrived at the edges of the fields, and tears that fell along the river's edge.

These lives of ours, the dailiness, the mundane as well as the extraordinary, inform our writing lives. How could they not?

We are firmly into sweater season. I find myself reaching for one every morning when I get dressed, I no longer have to check the weather to see if the extra layer is appropriate. Instead, I check the weather to see how many shirts to put underneath. After reaching for the same one a few days in a row, I take a good look at my sweater cabinet.

The deeper I dig, the more surprises I find. The sweater knitting flurry of last winter pays off, as I'm reacquainted with garments I only had a chance to wear once or twice before the seasons changed. It's like seeing long-lost friends, each one with their personality and attributes, all made by my own two hands. Bits of memories flit across my mind of hours spent knitting by the fireplace and in my green chair while watching TV at night with Lucas. Holding them in my hands, it feels like each stitch represents a hope or wish I had for this year, for where I am now. I start to wonder how this year holds up against those hopes, and even with the ups and downs and changes in plans, I firmly believe the year surpassed all I had imagined for 2023. Hopes are different from expectations, and I find that my hopes are always more simple and truthful than even the smallest expectation I might hold.

The reintroduction of all the sweaters brings with it

291

a renewed adoration of more complicated knitting projects. Instead of the basic sock pattern I've knit half a dozen times in the last few weeks using smooth sock yarn that makes stitches that fly off the needles, I'm drawn to a more rustic yarn - Lettlopi Icelandic wool in particular - that I bought earlier in the year when Mom and I had our getaway down at the coast, and we talked more than we shopped in the yarn store.

I search through patterns to find just the right mitten pattern, something that stretches my skills just enough, on mid-size needles that can be whipped together in a weekend. It doesn't take me long to find a one that ticks all the boxes - the Talvi Mittens by Kajsa Vuorela Fredriksson. It includes a snowflake motif on the front of the mitts and a simple repetitive design across the palms. It doesn't take me long to cast on, and in no time I'm enjoying working multiple strands of the rustic yarn at once. The complexity of following the pattern is enough to quiet the part of my brain that sometimes will not stop, the part that draws me down rabbit holes and to distraction, the part that won't let me feel ease.

But now, I'm feeling ease in buckets.

The mitts take no longer than a weekend, and my hands are itching for another, more substantial project. I think of my sweater cabinet and start to wonder what I'd like to add to the collection. Earlier in the year when I was working through my wardrobe/identity crisis I started focusing on wearable pieces, and I want to continue choosing projects in that same vein. I scroll through the patterns I have in my Ravelry library and find the Cargill Sweater by Rebecca Clow. It's a raglan sweater with an all-over dip stitch pattern, and I've had yarn for it squirreled away for quite some time. The pattern looked simple enough, but the stitch pattern spread over the raglan increases means you have to add to the pattern as you go, using that part of my brain that just didn't want to be used for weeks if not months.

But now, with the boost I've had with the mittens, I feel ready to tackle just such a project. I dig out the yarn, a silk mohair, and a wool fingering weight - both in a soft blue - that will be held together, needles, print the pattern, and get to work.

The cast-on and set-up rows take me three tries, I can't seem to get the stitch counts right, but I'm not deterred. The patience I need is within, and I smile as I cast on for the fourth time. Forget the third time being the charm, I love even numbers so there's something about the fourth time that I know will be the one.

There's something about being in a moment of deep concentration, maybe close to flow, where setbacks are seen as a challenge and not a problem that builds strength, even resilience. These are the moments to look back on when we're in the midst of overwhelm and angst. These are the moments that make us pick up our work again, even when, maybe especially because we know it will not always be smooth sailing but we can persevere.

Once I see the pattern coming together and know the rhythm of the stitches and the rate of increases, my shoulders pull down from my ears and I put my work on my lap and smooth down the fabric. It's beautiful. The dip stitches are made by knitting into a few rows beneath your working stitches, and you pull up the yarn on either side which creates little heart shapes as well as pillows of air within the stitches. Combined with the softness of the silk mohair, I already know this will be one of my most worn sweaters as soon as it's off the needles. The stitch pattern grows slowly, so this will not be a sweater completed in two weeks, it will be a long but enjoyable process. It will be one worked in the background during the upcoming holiday festivities, during the menu planning of Thanksgiving, and making lists of gifts for Christmas. It's a constant, this project, and just like the mitts, it requires just enough attention to quiet the anxious part of my mind, and fill it with purpose and concentration.

At the same time that I'm drawn deeper into knitting projects, I pick up work on the novel again. I'm craving more edits and more time with the characters. The story takes place during the winter months, and so it's no surprise to me that I want to get cozy in my work as well as at home. I'm drawn in particular to scenes that take place by a wood stove or out in the snow-covered pines.

It seems this time of year, possibly invigorated by the cold, I have the brain power and energy for things beyond what's directly in front of me. My mind can work out problems in the background in ways it hasn't for the last few months.

By mid-month, I'm working through plot holes and firming up character development at rapid speed. The story is in the background as I knit the dip stitch patterned sweater, and I find myself jotting down notes or running to the computer to change details.

This is again why life and writing are linked - they happen at the same time, constantly. There is no off button for writers. We get ideas in the shower, while making dinner, and while working our day job. At the most inopportune times we'll shout out "That's it!" or "YES!" and the people around us have no idea what's happening. We live our stories in our heads while we're living our own lives in real-time. There's a duality that is mind-bending and surreal.

And it's why I believe so many creative folks are drawn to nature, to the outdoors. We need something to ground our bodies and minds, a respite for our souls. And there is nothing like being in fresh air to find clarity, and calm, and to reset our senses. It's also why repetitive and meditative tasks are so important. As I noticed earlier in the month with my knitting, we - and not just creative folks, people in general - need ways to occupy different parts of our brains for other parts to do their thing. Maybe it has something to do with how our brains are being rewired and our attention spans changed thanks to our current digital age, but then again I'm willing to bet we've always needed different types of mental stimulation.

Whatever combination is at play, the third draft of the novel is completed by mid-month. Once I started, I couldn't stop. It felt good to be in the midst of the story, it felt satisfying to go through chapters methodically and make changes, and it felt like a contented sigh to share the story with two early readers for another round of feedback before deciding what path this story needs to take next.

The shift in energy this month feels a bit like that of the busy squirrels and chipmunks outside storing food for winter. It's a little more hurried than usual, but methodical and steady with the slowness and chill of the coming season right around the corner. Dad mows the wildflower meadow down and Lucas, Dad, and Fynn make wooden guards to protect the rhododendrons from the snow. And when the sunshine finds its way into the house it shows off the cobwebs and warms the floors and reminds us that there's nuance in the weather and our days and lives.

Our morning walks quickly become frost-covered. Today we notice the frost line shifting and then disappearing with the sun. Standing still you can see the nearly imperceptible shift in front of your eyes.

From mid-month on there's a flurry of activity at
our house. Fynn's birthday comes, finishing up this season
of birthdays, as does Mary Lou's arrival for a Thanksgiving
visit. We celebrate Fynn's seventeen years gathered around
our dining room table. Mary Lou, Mom, and Dad join
us and our singing voices send Darcey under the table,
but Fynn smiles and blows out the candles that sit on the
cake Paige baked for him. There's a voice missing, and
we tell the story of how Ted was the first one to visit Fynn
in the hospital after he was born. We'll probably tell the
story every year from now until forever. It's how we keep
memories alive, through stories. And we're so grateful we
have so many.

The Tuesday before Thanksgiving we take our
usual morning walk a little later than normal. Just as we're
coming up Sledding Hill Darcey stops to sniff at a bunch
of leaves. I stop and wait while she explores, and it dawns
on me how quiet it is. It's been weeks since we heard the
buzzing of any sort of insects, and unlike weekends and
early mornings, there haven't been any gunshots. Even the
crinkle of leaves beneath our feet is dwindling in favor of a

cushion of pine needles now that the leaves have started to break down and decompose. Our days are becoming more quiet as well. While there are preparations to be made for the holidays, there's also more space for chats over cups of tea with Mom, and afternoons feel wide open for knitting and reading for pleasure. After what seems like months of going at warp speed in one way or another, the slower pace is a welcome change. We're no longer gathering for winter, we've finished with most of our appointments and obligations aside from the dailiness of school work for the kids and both my and Lucas's work routines, the yard and fields are ready for snow, and we're just about ready to sit back and enjoy the upcoming hibernation.

Overnight it snows three inches. I wake up with another cold, so we postpone our Thanksgiving gathering until Saturday. I spend the day in bed, trying to stay away from the family so as not to get anyone else sick. We wait for the snow to turn to rain, and it does - but eventually, it ends up going back to snow. From my bed, I watch out the window as fat flakes fall from the sky.

On Thanks • ⮾ ⟶ ᴋts from next door wishing us a happy holiday. It's the first Thanksgiving in my memory where I can't smell turkey roasting in the oven - and it's not just because of my stuffy nose. Lucas takes the kids down to the coast to spend the day with Mary Lou.

Instead of turning on the Macy's Parade, I sit and watch my family prepare to leave. They promise to text me throughout the day. After I hear the car leave the driveway I get myself some breakfast, take a shower, and then tend to the one thing I've been waiting to do for weeks: getting out the Christmas mugs.

We've amassed a collection over the years, and have nearly enough to fill our mug rack that hangs on the kitchen wall. Darcey pads alongside me as I head down to the basement and grab an armload of mugs, she looks at me with curiosity as I switch out our daily mugs for festive ones.

I expect to feel sad and melancholy today without Lucas and the kids. We've been together on this holiday for years on end, whether we were at home or visiting extended family. I expect to feel guilty about having to postpone our celebration.

To my surprise, I feel a sense of acceptance that washes over me as I drink my herbal tea out of a candy cane-striped mug and settle into a day of knitting and reading in my favorite chair.

As with so much of this last year, things look different. And different is okay. It doesn't mean there's any less love being shared or less thanks extended, there isn't less of anything. If anything, there's more. More gratitude, more grace, more love.

On Saturday when we celebrate Thanksgiving with parts of our extended family, there's less pressure than on the actual holiday. It's like we took the self-imposed stress away by choosing a day that worked better for us, instead of sticking to our man-made calendar.

It's brisk outside, and we decide to finally light the fireplace for the first time this season. Lucas gets a roaring fire going, and the house feels cozier than usual within minutes. The heat pumps can't be compared to that of the wood stove. The warmth from the fire feels primal and ancient, like bringing the outdoors inside.

The day is full of food, including pumpkin pies

made from a pumpkin my mother grew in her garden, and gravy made from her Perfect Gravy recipe that lives in a cookbook she created for me and Toby when we moved out on our own. It's a day spent together quietly, while it's not the first Thanksgiving spent in our house, it's the first time Mary Lou has joined us here for a holiday. And it's the first big one without Ted. The lack of his presence is felt in the pauses, in the heart sighs. And yet there are still plenty of moments of levity. The turkey finishes in the oven nearly two hours ahead of schedule and there's a scramble - as there is every year - to finish all the sides so everything is still hot when it arrives on the table. Both of the grandmothers end up sitting on our living room couch shouting at the Ohio State and Michigan football game. We eat too much pie and the dishes stack high on the kitchen counter and there isn't enough room in the refrigerator for all the leftovers.

After we say goodbye to grandparents traveling near and far, the four of us retreat to our favorite corners of the house and don't speak a word for hours, we simply rest in the post-holiday glow and let all the moments percolate and integrate.

It snowed just enough for flakes to nestle into dried blades of grass. As we walk down Chickadee Lane, Lucas stops and points to a pile of pine cone seeds. It looks as though someone sat in the middle of the path and ate the entire thing, leaving the husks behind in a neat pile. It makes me think about how this time of year so often we've prepared for winter, and finally have a moment to rest.

It's final day of November. Lucas has a meeting he has to prepare for, so it's just me and Darcey on the morning stroll. We take our time. Everything smells different when frozen, which means Darcey sniffs everything twice, thoroughly. We pass Chickadee Lane, opting instead for a walk down to and around Lower Field. The ground beneath my feet feels solid, even the ridges made by tractor tires stand firm and don't crumble with my weight. The wind that's whipped through the fields and our bones the past few days has died down, and as I stand out in the open with the warmth of the sun on my face and cold air in my lungs, I feel a profound sense of being where I belong.

As we walk around the far corner of the field, I

catch glimpses of the river through the trees. There are bits of ice floating on the current, and the edges of the river are starting to freeze.

Darcey pauses behind me. I look back at her to see she's watching something far off in the distance. It's a deer, in the middle of the field. Both of us stand still in wait. The deer stands tall, ears alert, but unmoving. I'd like to think it's the one we've seen up by the houses, and in the field just past Mom and Dad's house.

I've wondered about it, as it's still deer hunting season and we haven't seen it for a while. A few weeks ago a young man showed up in our driveway, asking if we were the ones who posted the no trespassing signs, if that was our property that abutted the river. I told him we were, and it is. You don't hunt back there? He asked. No, I told him, we don't. He told me he'd been tracking a big deer that crossed the river onto our property, his voice trailed off into an unspoken question. I said I'm sure it did, it's a safe place back there. Then I told the young man good luck wherever else he ends up and he slunk back to his truck, shoulders slumped.

Darcey and I continue to watch the deer until it catches wind of us, and it turns and leaps across the field and into the swampy area, its white tail bounding gracefully.

"Let's go," I tell Darcey, smiling to myself with the knowledge that the deer survived the last few months. As we cross the field and walk up Sledding Hill towards home, there's a warmth in my chest as I think about the way this land, this space, has been a haven for me and the shifts of the months and seasons within as well as all that's encompassed in the landscape.

It's a humble plot of land, but it encompasses and represents more and more as our time on and with it grows. We're forging not only our own paths but a relationship with our surroundings. It's funny what sometimes brings about the feeling of kinship, a moment when we stand firm in our boundaries, an awe-filled encounter with a deer in the field, or when we are covered in soot cleaning the chimney, but the house and the property feel more alive every day. And in turn, so do we.

December

It's the first of December, and our Christmas tree sits by the fireplace with only lights draped around its branches.

Yesterday we went out back at lunchtime and chopped down the Christmas tree. We'd planned on bringing it in this weekend, but with inclement weather on the horizon, we decided not to wait any longer.

The four of us, plus the dog, crunched our way across the frozen ground, work gloves and electric chainsaw in hand. It didn't take long. We'd already tagged it weeks ago, and with the muscle that comes with teens, Lucas and I didn't even need to carry the tree home. It sat between the kitchen and the sitting room for the remainder of the day, unadorned.

"I'm in no rush," I told everyone.

But by the evening, the promise of cozy Christmas lights won me over.

"Let's just do the lights," I said.

So we brought up the box of lights from the basement and found one single ornament on top. Like always, it was the last one off last year's tree, tucked so far into the branches that we didn't find it until we took the lights off. Until it was nearly too late.

We wrapped the lights around the twiggy branches, and by the time we finished, our hands were covered in sap.

I looked over at the lone ornament and paused to consider how simple and elegant it looked with just the lights.

But then I decided the little ceramic heart needed to be the first ornament, the lovebirds singing from the branches, reminding me of our first holiday together all those years ago. Our humble origins, that second-floor apartment on Ropes Street, how we merged our ornaments and lives so quickly because we couldn't not.

There's a second ornament up now, too. It's our yearly one where we list our family members' names, including the dog and two rabbits, and the year. There's a sweetness to these two, where we've come from and our present. The in-between moments hold so many memories and stories.

I'm sitting here now, pausing with my tea, toying with the idea of leaving the tree with lights and two ornaments. If I didn't know the stories of the countless ornaments down in the basement, I might leave it. But I'm greedy for memories that flood the senses as we unwrap each bauble and trinket, and know we'll have the tree fully decorated soon. For now, it's perfect.

Early in the month, Mom invites Paige and me to a wreath making class at the UMaine Extension in Yarmouth. Tables are set up with piles of greens and a wire wreath form. We're lined up, me, Paige, and then Mom. Paige is by far the youngest in the group, but Mom's not the oldest. We're in a high tunnel, and while it's brisk outside the sun is shining and I find myself taking layers off as the workshop moves forward. Our hands are sticky with sap, but all of us enjoy working with our hands. We are three generations of crafters, and I know the line goes further back. Mom and I both watch Paige and marvel over her creation, how she's taken to yet another new craft. She's the kind of person who picks up things easily, and has a knack for just about anything she tries. Her mind works quickly, and with youth her hands are more agile than either of ours. At the end of the class we stand together, the three of us, holding up our wreaths as the instructor takes our photo. Later, when I'm looking at the photo, I can see the threads between us, the way we are tied together by genetics and love and these shared experiences we intentionally create.

The following day we're due to get our first real snowstorm of the season. Last month's snow was an appetizer, the upcoming six to eight inches is the main course. The day starts with Lucas running out to the grocery store for our weekly shop, and then some to-do's around the house. It's one of those days where one thing flows into the next, and before you know it you're elbow-deep in house projects and laundry. But then, early afternoon, the snow starts. We start a fire, Lucas turns on a football game, and Paige and I make a batch of Christmas Brownies. They're from Mom's cookbook, and she calls them Sugared Brownies because she would cut them up, and then roll each one in sugar. I omit that step and call them Christmas Brownies because even without the sugar, thanks to the amount of butter included they are more of an indulgence than the super easy brownies I make on a whim throughout the year.

After we pop them in the oven, as soon as I sit down on the couch, hot tea in hand, I look outside. It's calling to me. I ask the kids if they want to go for a snowy walk with me and Darcey. As they start to get ready to go outside I forget about the hot cup of tea, start putting on my layers, and call out to Lucas to take the brownies out of the oven when the timer goes off.

It's the first day after deer hunting season, so we don't put Darcey on a leash. We head out back, and she stays right next to us for the first part, but by the time we head down the hill towards Upper Field, she's sniffing all the things and exploring a little bit farther. On Hobbit Hill I look behind me and see Paige with her phone out, looking at the snow that's landed in her hair. The weight of the flakes has matted down her curly bangs, and she laughs so hard she nearly falls over. Fynn and I share a smile, there's nothing like hearing Paige's laughter float around you.

We decide to walk the Bucket Trail, where snow falls in some spots and not in others, depending on the thickness of the foliage and evergreens. The sky is overcast and gray, the trail is dim and it looks as though it's much later in the afternoon than it is. But the spots where the snow has made it to the ground look like they're illuminated.

"It looks like there should be a sword in the stone over there," says Paige, pointing to an open area in the woods where there's a downed tree and a sprinkling of snow.

The river is calm, but it puckers as though it's being pelted by raindrops. The snow falls in thick, wet, heavy clumps that splash upon meeting the water.

Once we're back in the field, Darcey runs up ahead to find the path back towards Sledding Hill. We call her back and she runs towards us, sliding in right beside me as if she were skidding into home base, her tongue lolling, flecks of snow bright against her dark fur. For the rest of the way home, we play that game - she runs up ahead and then turns around and comes back to us. She loves the freedom of being off-leash, but more so, she loves the snow.

Back at home, I put my mug of tea in the microwave as the kids start the kettle for cups of hot chocolate.

I can't stop smiling at the falling snow, the smell of holiday baking, the warmth of the fire. It's absolute perfection, and I'm swimming in disbelief that this is our life. There isn't a single spark of anxiety in my heart, no case of the Scary Sundays in sight.

I'm fully in this moment with my family. Here. And it's more than enough.

We wake up to over six inches of wet, heavy snow. It clings to every tree branch in sight, and outside it looks like a Thomas Kincaid painting. Late in the morning Lucas and I head out with Darcey. Early this morning she wanted to stay out and play in the snow, but it was time for breakfast and waking up slowly and hot mugs of tea. Now's the time, we tell her, and as soon as we step outside she jumps in the snow, and then digs around with her snout, coming up with the sweetest doggy grin on her face. In no time she's run around and collected so much snow in her fur that it looks as though she's wearing floaties on her arms like a toddler does in a swimming pool, or that she has giant snow muscles bulging from her extremities. Every so often we stop her and try to brush the attached balls of snow away. They must be pulling on her fur something fierce, but she doesn't seem to mind.

"I think I won," says Lucas.

There's clearly more than six inches, and the closest date on the Liquid Crystalline Prognosticator Extraordinaire prediction list is his. For the second time in three years, he'll be using the mug we've allocated as a prize until the spring equinox.

We make our way around the normal route, pausing whenever Darcey wants to play. It's a workday, but Lucas is in no rush to get back to his desk. His eyes dance just as much as mine do as we look around at the trees that are so heavy with snow that they bend over creating archways. Down on Chickadee Lane, where the path is normally clear and open, we have to crouch beneath bent tree branches, climbing through openings as if we're going through a portal into the North Pole or Narnia.

All is quiet except for the sound of snowplows in the distance. It's still snowing, just heavier than a flurry.

We're in awe of the early snowfall, and it reminds me of how much is out of our control. Weather often does that. I have a deep aversion to checking the weather past a day or so, because there's nothing I can do about it, and it only causes me to worry about if I'll have to change plans, or not. During our first two winters here there were many times when the forecast would predict inches and inches of

snow, we'd make preparations and get ahead of ourselves
only to be left with a dusting and disappointment.

But this storm proves that sometimes the forecast is
spot on. With Dad using his tractor to clear our driveway,
both Lucas and myself working from home, and the kids
not having to worry if the buses are running to school, there
isn't the pressure of getting on the road for a commute.
We have the privilege of staying safe and warm, our day
continues without much change regardless of the weather.
We get to choose how much we want to interact with the
outdoors, and how, aside from a bit of necessary shoveling.

This privilege of course changes how we feel about
snow. It's less an inconvenience, and more an invitation
to slow down and pause, to go deeper within to allow
ourselves to enjoy what's right in front of us.

Later in the day, Mom leaves a box on our doorstep
for Lucas. In it is the Liquid Crystalline Prognosticator
Extraordinaire mug filled with battery-powered twinkle
lights and tissue paper. I bring it in and try to show Lucas,
but he's in a meeting. I leave it on the kitchen counter,
twinkle lights aglow, and settle into my spot on the couch

in front of the fire. An hour or so later Lucas walks into the room holding his award, the glow from the mug lights up his face - as does his smile. He doesn't say much about it, but I know he appreciates the thoughtful silliness at the core of this ceremonial gift.

The week continues, and the weather stays consistent after the snowfall. It's cold and there's barely any wind, allowing for the snow to remain flocked on the trees for days after the storm.

I take an opportunity to look through my notebooks and try to wrap my head around my writing life this past year. It's been consistent, productive, and full of learning. I've written most weeks of the year, if not daily, whether journaling, on this project, or the novel. There have been breaks, but it's the most consistent I've been in recent years. There's something to be said for that, in showing up for yourself and your work.

The words are still coming, but this month I can feel the pressure being taken off the gas. I've hunted and gathered and stored, maybe there's room for a little bit of play in the snow. Maybe there's room for getting lost in thought. Maybe there's room for silliness and joy and indulgence. Maybe there's room to roll around in the snow and revel in the words written and the joys held and the hardships overcome.

Exactly a week after the snowstorm that landed us in a snow globe for the better part of a week, it's a dreary Monday. Overnight we had a few inches of rain, and the storm lingers with wind and drizzle. The sky is a dark gray, not the hopeful gray of last week's storm, full of bright excitement. Nonetheless, Darcey is desperate for a walk, and so I take her out on my own. The two of us bundle up, me in my L.L.Bean jacket and secondhand boots, her in a cute little puffy coat I picked up for her the other day. It's bright blue and green, and since we're out of hunting season, it's acceptable. She doesn't need a coat, her fur is thick and warm, but it helps us to keep track of her, and also helps the snow from sticking in all the places like it did last week.

The snow has fallen or melted completely from the trees. The world no longer looks like a winter wonderland. Now the muddy ground squishes beneath my boots with each step, and I walk carefully as there's hardly any snow to cushion my fall. This scene is partly why I know so many people dislike winter. This is the part that makes us dig deep and find beauty in the mud. We have to try a little harder when the snow melts and we're left with piles of sandy ice and gray sludge. Even the wreaths on our doors look a little downtrodden.

I look up from my desk when I realize the room has grown a bit dark, and there's a blizzard outside. Earlier in the day there were blue skies, but now all I can see are snowflakes rushing past and pelting the window. It's so unexpected that it makes me laugh out loud to myself, startling Darcey. I've been complaining about how the snow that's left behind from the last storm looks tired, and how there isn't anything in the forecast.

Leave it to the great state of Maine and Mother Nature to surprise me.

A few moments later it turns to hail, and then to what looks like styrofoam balls bounce when hitting the ground, and then it turns back to snow that seems furious. In German, there's a word for this - graupel, which means soft hail, or snow pellets.

The driveway is covered in moments, and the snow changes once more to big clumps of fluff that dance on the wind. The way the clusters swoop and lower reminds me of a ballet, I wonder how well this dance I'm witnessing would pair with the Nutcracker.

Almost as soon as it started, the storm is gone again. Snow lingers on the grass, but leaves puddles in the driveway, the blacktop a danger zone of liquid left to mix with frigid temperatures.

The next day, the temperatures drop. Out on the edges of Lower Field, the quarter inch of snow lays pristine, aside from animal tracks. From what I can see there are rabbit, deer, and maybe coyote tracks. In the middle of the field it looks like a deer marched out, and nestled into the snowy ground, probably days ago when there was still a good amount of snow. There are mounds pushed aside as if she shimmied her body into comfort.

Snow pellets are mixed in with the snow and pine needles, and when I step, the ground seems to give, but it's the layers of snow, thin ice, and frozen leaves that crunch and give way beneath my feet.

Earlier in the month Paige and I were out shopping and came across a display of candles. We were in no hurry, so we smelled all of the different scents, showing each other our favorites. Paige held one in her hand, sniffed, and gasped. "It smells like Papa," she said, handing me the candle.

We bought it, because how could we not?

Now it sits on the top of a pie chest filled with craft supplies in our kitchen, and each morning as I walk past it I catch a hint of pipe tobacco I smile as I think of Ted, sitting on a porch and leaning back in his chair, sunglasses on, one leg crossed over the other, looking out at either the ocean or their woods in New Hampshire where they lived before becoming snowbirds. He used to sit so still that hummingbirds would come to visit him.

Sometimes I catch Lucas in the same spot with a sad smile. I don't ask what he's thinking, though. We've found that grief is as private as it is communal, in separate and individual moments.

It's Sunday, a week and a day until Christmas.
We've heard shots go off somewhere in the distance, and
while Darcey has managed them okay in the house, she
refuses to go out on our daily walk around the property. But
since I've already got my coat and boots, I decide to go out
by myself.

As I walk around both Lower and Upper Fields, I
keep looking up at the birch trees, thinking I catch glimpses
of birds sitting on empty branches. The closer I get, I find
that they're just clumps of dry leaves, bound in cobwebs
or some other material. But from a distance, you'd never
know. Today the temperatures are rising, but the river
flooded earlier in the week and there are traces of how the
water froze after the flood but before it receded, there's ice
left all over. I can hear branches or acorns falling on top of
the ice, tinkling as they drift away from their rooted homes.
I leave footprints in inches of snow that will disappear by
tomorrow when we're met with another rain storm. We're
in a cycle that's familiar from last December: snow, rain,
ice, melt, snow, repeat.

Always changing, always unknown even in its

familiarity. Something is always disappearing just as soon as it's arrived.

In the middle of the fields, there are crater-like indents in the ground, and when it floods, these areas fill with water, freeze, and then when the water recedes there's a thin layer of ice left behind atop a field of green grass. I walk across and the ice cracks before my foot presses down. Crack crack crack. It's satisfying knowing that I can step through and my foot will be met with spongy earth without fear of slipping. And yet it makes me think of the spring when I spent the better part of May in bed recovering from the concussion. How unsteady I was for weeks and what felt like months and still the reminder lingers. As I look around the field I think about the year, the surprises it's brought, both good and bad. The consistency of some things, the upheaval in other areas. The constancy of the paths outside that called to us in all weather, the way the land has held our footprints and streams of tears, our grief and joy, our laughter and tense words. It's there through it all.

Back at home, there are telltale signs of December: cookie dough chilling in the fridge, a late-season football game on the TV in the living room, and a few stray gifts in the bedroom closet waiting to be wrapped and set under the tree. With fresh air still clinging to my reddened cheeks, I step inside the warmth of the house and feel the words of Robert Frost, "And miles to go before I sleep, and miles to go before I sleep," deep down into my core. Such is December.

Later that night the wind starts to howl, and the rain begins in full force. We fall asleep listening to the storm, curtains drawn and blankets up to our chins, hoping for it to sound worse than it is.

The next morning, just as I'm finishing up in the shower, the power goes out. With no electricity, there's no wifi, and with no wifi, there's little Lucas can do for work. So we take our plans for the day and throw them out the window and into the wind, which is still gusting and blowing harder than we've ever seen. The temperatures are mild, but still, we start a fire. A text rolls in from my parents, asking if we also lost power. Within a few hours, they've got their generator going, and have offered their bathroom and anything else we need. While they've had a generator for years, we have yet to make that investment.

It can't go on that long, we tell ourselves. We'll be

fine.

Still, we bring up a stash of plastic water bottles from the basement and grab five-gallon water jugs from my parents to flush our toilet.

Darcey paces the house a bit, unsure of the sound the trees are making. Lucas takes her outside to pee and comes in shaking his head, his eyes wide. "It's like the trees are clapping together, it's an awful sound," he tells me. We don't go out for our daily walks, instead, we try to keep ourselves busy with books and projects that don't need electricity. We all take naps. I read half a book in the afternoon until the light fades. It's been dark all day due to storm clouds, but there are still hints of light. I move around the sitting room finding pockets of it to read by, until finally my eyes are weary and strained and I put the book down instead of finding a flashlight.

I'm curled up on the couch by the fire, a blanket over me for comfort more than warmth, and just before I close my eyes and let slumber take over, I look out the windows and watch the trees in furious movements. The sound is as Lucas said, awful. It's a combination of trains rushing by and destruction. I shudder just as I'm overwhelmed by fatigue.

A while later I wake up, my eyes dart open, feeling

as though something is wrong.

It's silent.

No wind. No hum of electricity or anything. No trees clapping together. No traffic. No crackle of the fire, as it's just about gone out while I slept. Just silence. Endless silence.

Once we get the fire going again, and everyone congregates in the sitting room, I tell them I've got an early Christmas gift for everyone. After rooting around the gifts under the Christmas tree I find the one I have in mind. Paige opens it up to find Cards Against Humanity, a raunchy game that's a bit risqué, but I have a feeling it'll get us all laughing.

We light candles and start shuffling the cards, and in no time we're all bent over with laughter, tears streaming down a few of our faces. Lucas shakes his head and laughs harder than I've seen him in months. There's levity in the air, and even amidst the vulgar words and ridiculous card pairings, there's healing in the laughter.

Midway through the game Dad calls and lets us know, again, we can use their house for anything we need.

Watching my family around me, their faces illuminated by
the candles, Darcey sitting at our feet, there's nothing we're
lacking.

Before he goes to bed, Lucas takes Darcey out once
more. He comes inside and instead of talking about the
sound of the trees, he tells me to look outside at the clear
and cloudless night. Without the light pollution, even here
- miles away from a city - the sky is endless with too many
stars to count.

The kids and I stay up late since we've got nowhere
to be and nothing to do in the morning. Today was their
first official day of winter break, and both of them have
been looking forward to lazy mornings spent sleeping as
long as they like. Whenever the three of us sit around the
fire, we get silly, irreverent, and downright honest. We tell
stories and ask questions, we share jokes and memes, even
as the power from their phones dwindles. With candlelight
illuminating their faces, I see shadows of who they are,
who they've been, and who they're both becoming. I get
teary multiple times, but shake it off as Paige tells another
joke, or Fynn delivers the most unexpected one-liners that

leave me breathless with laughter. More core memories. It's a gift to notice them as they're happening.

We go to sleep feeling safe in our home, even without power. The temperatures stay mild, the wind continues to be still, and though there's some water in the basement and a leak or two in the attic from where the water came in sideways with gusts of wind, we're together, safe and warm, and counting our blessings.

On Tuesday morning we wake up to the hum of generators coming from all sides of our house, and bright sunshine. Lucas and I walk next door to make hot tea and oatmeal, and as we make our way up the driveway to Mom and Dad's we look around to assess the damage. We're not the only ones, across the street a half dozen people are looking at an open roof on an established barn where roof panels no longer sit. There are branches strewn across our yard, but aside from the water in the basement and leaks, we've got minimal damage compared to many. Most of the state of Maine is still without power, and the power company says that in some cases, it could take upwards of six days to restore electricity.

We read online that the rivers are reaching historic highs. We're still in the cycle I noted the other day, snow, rain, ice, melt, snow, repeat. We're through with the rain, and are waiting for the ice. We haven't had to worry about pipes bursting, but the freezing temperatures loom in the distance and we hope the power will come back on before the deep chill finds us.

When we go for our walk, we decide to skip Chickadee Lane and go down to look at the river. As we step into Upper Field, we hear the river loud and clear, we know it's close before we see it.

As we turn the corner, Lucas and I both gasp, the river is now where Lower Field was. We stand in awe at the edge of the field and river. In an instant, I'm transported back to May, back to the floods that I thought of just the other day, back to the spring of my concussion.

It's not just the field, the woods to our right are flooded as well. There is no Bucket Trail, only water, and by the look and sound of it, a fast-moving, deep body of water at that.

We backtrack and go down Chickadee Lane, marveling at the water that's risen halfway up the slope between the trail and the field that's covered in woods, but we can't make it around the trail, as it's flooded near the brush and wood chip pile. We turn around again, Darcey at our heels, and stop at Hobbit Hill to take in the view before exploring further.

Everything is underwater, so much more so than it was in May.

We walk down the Sledding Hill as far as we can, but again, we're cut off by water. There's a constant conversation between the two of us, shock and wonder laced with profanities because we're dumbstruck, awestruck, and everything in between.

Up the hill to the cabin we go, where we inspect the far side of Lower Field we couldn't see from any other viewpoint. Like everything else, it's underwater. But the sun is shining, and it glistens off the field-turned-lake, and through the far set of trees, we can see the original river, though it's wider than ever, how it's rushing and the way whitecaps are mixed with sunshine. It's stunning.

We walk back up to the houses, where we gather my parents, and walk back down so they can see the extent of the flooding. Fynn joins us, and Darcey is happier than she's ever been, herding the five of us as we walk. She jumps ahead, watches us coming, then runs to the back of the herd - where I am generally - and walks alongside me with her tongue hanging out. Then she's back up to the front, and back and forth she goes. Last night we noticed how she relaxed when we were all in the same room. Her instincts come into play, and when we're all in one spot for longer than a few minutes, her body sinks into the ground and sleep overcomes her in a way unlike any other time.

After hearing the grocery store has power, I make our way over to pick up a few things. We baked cookies on the weekend and had planned on icing them on Monday, but when the power went out those plans were extinguished. Now, as the reality sinks in that we may be without electricity for some time, we start to get creative. The icing recipe we use calls for melted butter (or in our case, dairy-free butter), confectioner sugar, vanilla, and whatever type of milk you use.

"We could make the icing on the stove," I say to Paige in a conspiratorial tone.

"Let's do it," she replies with a wide smile.

And so at the grocery store, we pick up the staples we need replenished and sprinkles from the baking aisle. As we drive to and from the store we note where the river has gotten high, nearly to the road, where the trees are down, what houses have their fire going with the telltale sign of smoke wafting from chimneys, and who's already started on yard cleanup.

At home, we get out the whisk instead of the electric mixer and get to work. We melt butter in a saucepan over the woodstove and then work quickly adding ingredients and whisking up the icing. When it starts to harden I plop the pan back onto the stove, get it soft again, and continue icing gingerbread and sugar cookies. We end up making three batches of icing to cover all of our cookies, and we ice and decorate them by candlelight as the afternoon light wanes. The dishes remain in the sink where they'll sit until we have running water, and we leave behind countertops covered in confectioner sugar and cookies.

Tonight, I start to feel the weight of it all. I feel the fatigue that comes from using every bit of energy as it takes four times longer and more steps to do just about everything. I feel the weight of the water in the basement. I feel Christmas looming, and the need to create magic moments for us all. I wonder how we'll do it, knowing that despite everything, we will.

I go to sleep more weary than I did the night before and sleep fitfully.

The next morning on the eve of the Winter Solstice, the kids and I prepare to leave the house for the day. The plan is for us to take Fynn to his Wednesday outdoor club, and Paige and I will go out to lunch for an actual meal in Freeport where there's electricity. From there we'll hang out at the library before meeting Fynn where we'll circle with other families who participate in the organization that leads his club, and gather for a solstice lantern walk. It's with a heavy heart that we leave the homestead, I feel torn leaving Lucas behind. There's work to be done, and as soon as we head out he and Dad bring the generator to our house. For the next few hours, he works on using the shop vac (which I had been explicitly told I would not be using, as we didn't need another concussion) to get rid of the water from the basement. He also washes all the dishes, cleans the kitchen, fills every water bottle we had, and prepares for the next bunch of unknowns as best he can.

I check my phone more than I should for updates, but when Paige and I sit down at the restaurant for lunch we look at each other and laugh because we're ravenous and my phone is forgotten. We both order protein-heavy meals, a burger for me and a Reuben sandwich for her. Our food is gone nearly as soon as it arrives. I don't remember a burger ever tasting so damn good.

Later we're at the library in comfy chairs, both scrolling on our phones. It feels like a luxury to be plugged into chargers, and mindlessly looking at Instagram. There's a pinch of guilt as Lucas texts to let me know he's finished all the work, but mostly I'm so filled with gratitude. I'm soaking in the time with Paige and the lights and the full belly.

Before we head home, we meet Fynn at Through the Trees for the lantern walk. He's with his group of friends but breaks free to say hi to us. I tell him to go back over and enjoy his time with them. Paige and I watch as families with small children arrive, their snowsuits and mittens bring back memories of long ago.

Then we begin. We walk out to an open field, lanterns of all types in our hands. Ours is a mason jar with a battery-operated candle inside. We walk through the woods to an open field where there's a spiral made of evergreens and twinkle lights, with a bonfire in the center. We walk the spiral single file and each drop a piece of birch bark infused with our intentions for the new year into the fire. Then we exit and stand in a circle around the spiral. Those who are leading the festivities give a few readings, there's movement and murmurs and wonder from the littlest in our midst. And then we lift our voices and all sing This Little Light of Mine.

Memories flood back of years past spent caroling at a monastery in Kennebunkport with my inlaws, of Lucas's strong voice singing out of tune but full of so much joy, the way Ted's face would light up as he watched the kids, mindful of the open flames of the candles they were holding, ever watchful and protective. How Mary Lou would wear the silliest headbands and hats along with Paige, both of their faces full of magic. The year we took my parents to the same event, something I'd wanted to do for years, and how my eyes teared up when I heard my father singing.

Allowing space for our past to infuse our present with meaning and memories enhances each moment and adds layers to our existence.

Now, flanked by my teenagers who are both taller than me, we're singing a song that is so simple, so pure, and so full of community and light. And my goodness, there is so much light.

Buoyed by the fresh air, the joyful voices, and a day that filled my cup in so many ways, we head home through the darkness, unsure of what will come next. With our usual route washed out and flooded, we have to drive home on unfamiliar roads, but eventually we make it home.

The garage door is open, waiting for us.

And as soon as we pull into the garage, the lights turn on.

The power is back.

Lucas opens the door, Darcey comes bounding out to greet us, and we are all whooping and hollering for the light.

The next few days are filled with clean-up and Christmas preparations, and they go by in a blink. The river recedes but leaves behind the same craters full of water that I stomped through when frozen a week ago. There are a few big trees that came down across the Bucket Trail, and the river brought sand well into the woods and field as it rushed past its capacity.

Lucas spends time in the basement, tending to waterlogged areas. There's a casing on the outside of the house that houses a bunch of wires, and at some point, it split due to being baked in the sun and then frozen for years, and he shuts the power off to patch it until we can have an electrician replace the whole thing.

Paige comes downstairs, "Why's the power out?" she asks, and I wonder if she expects the worst. But there's no fear in her voice, no annoyance. She trusts that we can handle whatever comes our way. When I tell her what her father is up to she nods and goes back to whatever it was she was doing.

On Christmas Eve Mom and Dad come over in the afternoon to join us on a video call with Toby and Adrienne. We wish them a Merry Christmas and tell them they need to come back over like they did last year, as we didn't bake nearly as many cookies without them. We share some excitement about my postponed trip that's now slated for the end of January. There's comfort in video calls, but it's nothing like a real hug, and I can't wait to hug them both. After the call, Dad heads home to make sticky buns for tomorrow's breakfast, but Mom stays to watch The Muppet Christmas Carol.

Mom picks a chair next to the Christmas tree, and the glow of the fireplace fills the room. She has a festive mug full of tea, and gingerbread cookies that were iced in the candlelight are now placed on a napkin draped over her lap. I'm sitting on the couch with a kid on either side of me, and as soon as the movie starts, I'm fighting back tears. Christmas is here. The familiar sounds and smells and sights and feelings surround me, and there's no fighting it. It came, even though we're still catching up from the week of unexpected power. Even though we miss loved ones. Even though we feel like our hearts can't take anymore, it's enough - all of it.

Christmas morning comes and while it's not a White Christmas, it's perfect. John Denver plays on the record player, there are thoughtful gifts exchanged, as well as the joyous mixture of laughter and tears. After we open presents and have breakfast with Mom and Dad, Darcey starts bouncing up and down, wishing and hoping on every jump for our regular walk. Lucas and I oblige and get bundled up, and we take our daily stroll.

There are gifts in the special, the holidays that punctuate the year, but there's also magic in the daily, the seemingly mundane, the routine.

The day passes gently, with a feast of lasagna with a cookie plate for dessert. There's love throughout and in the margins, gratitude in each line. Before the day ends I run my hands over the material gifts I've received: a handmade quilt covered in sheep made by my mother, a bowl turned by hand by my father made out of cherry, a stuffed "silly goose" crocheted by Paige to go along with an inside joke, a sketch of a chickadee in a birch tree by Fynn which he paired with a ceramic vase that's surface looks like birch bark, and a set of vintage dishes in the colors I adore, from Lucas. All the gifts were sourced or made locally, all brimming with creativity and thoughtfulness.

December has been a showcase for the generosity that comes from creativity. It has been present throughout the year, no doubt, but there is a giant spotlight on creativity this particular month. From curating experiences for our families to the thought that goes into gift-giving, even the simplest gesture stems from creativity. The definition of creativity includes "the use of imagination or original ideas." With that in mind, I would go a step further and say that love may be made up of creative energy. We show love in our own, unique ways. And through acts of love, connection and deep affection are born. They don't just happen, it takes work, thought, and intention. More than anything, I've learned that love and creativity work hand in hand.

Somewhere in the days between Christmas and New Year's that all blend, I finish the Cargill Sweater, the all-over dip stitch pattern I've worked on since the beginning of November. My mind is full of tying up writing projects and what comes next. Lucas has the rest of the year off from work, and the days pass in a continuous haze of sugar and Christmas specials on BritBox and meld into a solid mass where we can't distinguish which day of the week it is, as is the way of this last week of the year. We spend an evening at the Coastal Botanical Gardens in Boothbay for their Lights Aglow event, one of our gifts to Mom and Dad. It's a rainy evening, but we brave the weather with our raincoats. Mom and Dad wear their yellow slickers, and in a sea of black raincoats, they are our guiding forces. The botanical gardens are lit up in display after display, and again, there's laughter and light. So much light.

December light guides us to the new year, fuels us when we feel like we can no longer go on, and humbles us with the invitation to slow down, to fill even the hardened and aching corners of our hearts as full as can be before we hibernate.

On the last day of the year, the sun breaks through what has seemed like days of gray. We linger in the sunbeams, on the couch, by the fire. I know the day will unfold as it always does, with familiarity as well as unpredicted moments. Eventually, we'll head outside for our daily walk with Darcey, where we'll be met with frozen mud and fresh air, and birdsong. We'll check to see what the river is doing, and how much water is left in Lower Field. The kids will make their way downstairs with bedheads and bleary eyes, greeting the day in their way and their own time, wishing for these last days of winter break to extend further. We'll share meals and small moments. Lucas and I will steal kisses while passing each other in the kitchen. I'll jot down words to help me remember it all. There's a table tennis tournament slated for this evening, and after that, we'll put on a long and epic movie to help pass the last hours of this year.

And tomorrow, we'll begin again, this cycle of the year, of seasons. We'll uncover new growth, and new truths, on the well-trodden paths, and familiar ones on the previously untraveled.

When we close out the year, we're not saying goodbye. The days are continuous, our lives are as well, and while a year is a snapshot of a life, we're lucky that our days keep unfolding in front of us. The cycle continues. We feed our souls as best we can. We get tired. The rain comes and goes, the water rises and then falls, and the words fill my mind and spill over onto the page just as the floodwater breaks through the woods and into the fields. We hold tight to the ones we love, when they're here and when they're gone. We write each one of our days on the paths we walk, day after day. We work, we rest, we fill our cups, we give, we create, we love. Repeat. Repeat. Repeat.

Corinne Cunningham

Acknowledgements

The idea for Paths Through the Year was born alongside a hope for a different sort of creative process. I wanted to write a book in a way that shared the behind the scenes of writing, as well as the words in their raw state. I set out to share my process with others, and in doing so gained unexpected support and encouragement. Without these true patrons of the arts who gave so much more than financial support, this book might not be in your hands today! From the bottom of my heart, thank you to my beloved Patrons: Allison Hrip, Angela Vincent, Anna Maria Boland, Chrissy Vagenius, Deb Bird, Debra Smouse, Gina Darling Santangelo, Gina Kimmel, Grace VanAken, Jean Hare, Jen Precourt, Jennie Booth, Jenny Howard, Julie Canudo, Kate Coates Kim, Kate Roxburgh, Katie Li, Kim Nichols, Kylee Foote, Liz Vartanian, Loretta Marie Lupi-Lawrence, Mary Lou Cunningham, Michelle Ciani, Michelle GD, Michelle Halcomb, Michelle Lievense, Racquel Henry, Rochelle Butcher, Sarah Kennedy, Teresa Robinson, Toby M. Schreier, and Yao Li.

Thank you to the Confident Creative Club, the original and the spin off! When writers show up for each other and themselves true magic happens. Thank you for being a part of my writing life, and allowing me to be a part of yours.

To my circle of creatives I'm lucky to call friends, thank you for all the times over the last year and a half you've listened, shared, asked the perfect question, and commiserated with me! Specifically, gratitude to Mindy Tsonas Choi, Kylee Foote, Jessica Ray, Katie Li, and Michelle Ciani.

To Allison Hrip, thank you for how you held my hand through wobbles and explorations, how you mothered my writing soul in Asheville, at your kitchen table, and through squares on the computer!

Gina Kimmel, thank you for being my person, for understanding all the things I couldn't say but needed heard, and for being on this writing journey together. I can't wait to see where our words and friendship take us next.

To Toby M. Schreier and Adrienne Frie, thank you for being a part of this story, from near and far, in so many ways.

Mary Lou Cunningham, thank you for your support, enthusiasm, and participation. Ted, thank you for encouraging my writing. I will never forget how much it meant to me that you read Farm Girl, and asked for the next one. We will forever miss you and your reassuring presence.

Mom and Dad, thank you doesn't begin to scratch the surface! But still, thank you for saying yes to this wild adventure in Maine, for being the best neighbors, for reading early drafts, for letting me share you with the world, for allowing space when my head is still in my book worlds, and for giving me tools and stories to grow from the very beginning.

Fynn and Paige, thank you for allowing me to tell our stories. The love and grace you both have given me over the years means more than you'll ever know. Fynn, your map is such a perfect depiction of our homestead and serves as a compass, just as you do for our family. Paige, your illustrations and cover have given this book depth and beauty beyond the words on the page, much like you bring color and wonder to our lives. You two are my everything.

Last, but very not least, Lucas. Thank you for telling me to keep going. Thank you for your strong shoulders, your keen editing, for not batting an eye when I shared our arguments and tender moments on the page, and for always being my home. All my love, always.

Corinne Cunningham is a writer, mother, avid reader, knitter, and tea enthusiast. She lives with her family in the woods of Maine where she writes quiet stories full of heart. You can find her on Instagram at @crnnoel and updates on her website: www.corinnecunningham.com